THE O'DOWD

BY

DION BOUCICAULT,
Author of "Arrah-na-Pogue," "The Shaughraun,"
"The Colleen Bawn," "The Omadhaun,"
Etc., Etc.

Copyright, 1909, by Mrs. Josephine Cheney.

London:
SAMUEL FRENCH, Ltd.,
Publishers,
26, SOUTHAMPTON STREET,
STRAND.

New York:
SAMUEL FRENCH,
Publisher,
28, WEST 38th STREET.

THE O'DOWD.

Produced at the Adelphi Theatre, London, on October 21st 1880, with the following cast :—

Dennis O'Dowd	Mr. DION BOUCICAULT.
Mike	Mr. HENRY NEVILLE.
Bertie Talboys	Mr. E. COMPTON.
Colonel Muldoon	Mr. PROCTOR.
Romsey Leake	Mr. J. G. TAYLOR.
Lord Ossidew	Mr. NORMAN.
Borromore	Mr. ROBERTSON.
Chomley	Mr. GREGORY.
Chalker	Mr. R. PATEMAN.
Barney	Mr. FREW.
Mat	Mr. FOX.
Sligo Dan	Mr. ARCHER.
Mr. Daly	Mr. COOPER.
Wilcox	Mr. J. COOPER.
Lady Rose Lawless	Miss PATEMAN.
Mrs. Dudley Fowler	Miss OTWAY.
Mrs. Wilton Gore	Miss H. MATHEWS.
Kitty M'Coul	Miss LYDIA FOOTE.
Maud	Miss FRANKLIN.
Grace	Miss HODGES.
Bridget O'Dowd	Miss LE THIERE.
Miss Vansittar	Miss MELROY.

THE O'DOWD.

ACT I.

A Room in the Temple. Doors R.H. 2E., and L.H.U.E. Fireplace L. Window C. Curtains drawn. Bookcase and engravings against the walls. A secretary bureau R.H., 1 E. Card-table with candles R.H. Table with remnants of repast L.H., opposite fireplace. Decanters, bottles, glasses, cigar-boxes, photographs over mantelpiece amongst the ornaments. Several packs of cards lie on floor near table R.H., as if thrown there in disorder. Shaded lamps on mantelpiece and on piano.

MULDOON, MIKE, *and* OSSIDEW *playing at table* R.H. BORROMORE *stands behind* COL. MULDOON. TALBOYS *stands behind* MIKE. *Very light music.*

MUL. I raise it. Fifty.
BORRO. Percy will raise it a hundred.
MUL. One hundred and fifty.
OSSI. I pass. (BORROMORE *crosses to* L.C.)
MIKE. I see you! Two aces and three queens.
MUL. Two aces and three kings! I've the devil's own luck!
MIKE. How do I stand now, Talboys?
TAL. (*writing on a card*) You owe the colonel six hundred and twenty-five; and you owe his lordship two hundred and ten.

BORROMORE *crosses to table* L.H., *and helps himself to wine.*

MIKE. Bertie, you have taken away my brandy.
TAL. Yes; you have had enough!
OSSI. (*aside to* TALBOYS) Can't you leave him alone?
TAL. (*rises; goes to window* C.) No! He has been playing since midnight, and is losing heavily.
OSSI. Well, he can afford it! A few thousands more or less are no great matter to him. Perhaps you want him all to yourself? (*crosses to fireplace*)

TAL. Exactly! with a few feathers left on him to fly with. (*goes up and draws the curtains of window, letting in the daylight*) Gentlemen, it is past eleven o'clock. (*music ceases*)

OSSI. By Jove! It is time for breakfast. (*rises; crosses to* L.H.)

MUL. Shall we cut whether it is to be double or quits?

MIKE. Done!

MUL. The lowest wins.

MIKE. (*cutting the pack*) Three!

MUL. (*cutting*) Ace! It is wonderful!

MIKE. (*to* TALBOYS) How do I stand amongst you all?

TAL. (*looking at card*) It will take two thousand and fifty to cover it. (*goes to* L.E. *at back*)

MIKE. (*going to bureau* R.) If I draw the cheque for all my losses, will you kindly settle for me with Ossidew and Borromore?

MUL. I'll be your paymaster, me boy, with pleasure. (*crossing to* C., *sits* R. *of table* L.H.)

TALBOYS *crosses to door* R.U.E.

OSSI. Walsingham loses like a prince.

BORRO. No wonder—he is so beastly rich! What charming rooms you have here, Percy!

MUL. And what glorious parties he has given in them!

OSSI. (*at door* R.H.) Who is this fellow Michael O'Dowd, whose name figures here beside yours upon the door of these chambers? We have never seen him.

MIKE. He is rarely in town.

OSSI. He is Irish, of course?

MIKE. I believe so.

BORRO. (*who has been examining a photograph on the mantelpiece; goes to* C. *with photo*) Here is something that evidently belongs to him—the portrait of an old Irish bog-trotter. What is written here?—" Daddy sends his love to Mike," and signed " Kitty."

OSSI. (*who is looking at another photograph*) And here is Kitty—(*reads*)—" To Mike, from his own Kitty." She is charming! I wish I were Mike! (*down* L.H.)

MIKE. (*rising*) I shall feel obliged if you will replace those portraits where you found them. It seems to me dishonourable to enter thus into the life of a stranger, in whose rooms we happen to be guests.

OSSI. By Jove! he is right. (*replaces photo;* BORROMORE *does the same*)

MIKE *goes to* MULDOON *centre.* MIKE *hands* MULDOON *a cheque.*

Mul. When will I afford you a revenge for this? (*seated* L.C.)

Mike. (*goes to* R.H.) Never! Will you fill your glasses, gentlemen? (*all fill glasses at table* L.H.) We are here to-night that we might pass together the last hours that I shall spend in England.

All. No! You are not going to leave us?

Mul. Leave London in the middle of the season?

Ossi. Where you are knee-deep in a score of affairs of the heart?

Borro. Gentlemen, let us protest!

Mul. (*rises; goes behind table* L.H.) We will get a round robin signed by a score of the most photographic beauties. They shall issue out a *ne exeat* in the Court of High Life. This is treason!

Talboys *crosses at back to* R.H., *sits by desk* R.H.

Ossi. We cannot spare you, Walsingham.

Mike. Don't make my regret more painful. I assure you I have no choice; family affairs oblige me to go.

Mul. But you will return? The Duke expects you for the hunting season at the kennels.

Ossi. Lady Harrogate will never forgive you if you fail to put in an appearance at Bromley Moors.

Mul. Society has cast you for a leading part, and you dare to abscond?

Mike. Accept my grateful appreciation of the value you set on my fellowship. Ah, believe me, the loss is mine!

Mul. Gentlemen, are you charged? Allow me to speak in your names?

All. Hear! hear! Order! Hear the Muldoon!

Mul. Sir, Mr. Percy Walsingham—ahem!—at this late hour——

All. Early! Early!

Mul. I accept the amendment—at this early hour I will be brief, but sincere, sir. London society will share our regret when it hears it is about to lose not only one of the most wealthy but most distinguished of its members.

All. (*gently*) Hear! hear!

Mul. I repeat it!—(*fiercely*)—and I challenge dispute. Most distinguished, not only as a gentleman, but as a poet, whose name already stands at the head of the literature of the period!

All. Hear! hear!

Mul. And when a gentleman can stand being a poet he must be a gentleman of undisputed origin.

All. Hear!

MUL. When Mr. Percy Walsingham appeared suddenly amongst us two years ago, it was not by his wealth that he gained admission to our exclusive clubs, it was not the splendour of his life that raised him to a leading position in society—it was his brilliant wit, sir, in his charming address, sir, that we recognised the pedigree of the thoroughbred.
ALL. Hear! hear!
MUL. The Irishman, sir, has an eye for a gentleman and an eye for a horse. The nobleman of nature is a humbug, but the gentleman of race is undeniable! We are sorry to lose you from the stud!
ALL. Hear! hear! (ALL *get* C. *for hats and coats*)
MIKE. (*crossing to* L.H.) I wish you would not make it so hard for me to say "Farewell." I feel as if I were attending my own funeral. Yet I must say it; but, still, not yet. I need not bury myself now and here. We shall meet this afternoon at the garden party to which Lady Rose Lawless has invited us at Riverside, and to-night we shall meet at the club.
BORRO. We are deuced sorry that you are ordered off.
OSSI. It is an infernal nuisance to lose you.
MUL. We meet at the club to-night?
ALL. At the club to-night. (*exeunt* R.H.D. 3*rd*)

    TALBOYS *goes up to door, looks after them; closes door, crosses over to* L.H. *at back of table, to* MIKE *at fireplace.*

TAL. Percy!
MIKE. Yes!
TAL. You have met with some unexpected misfortune—there is something in my heart tells me that yours is in trouble.
MIKE. No; it is nothing—that I—could not foresee—it is inevitable—I have brought it upon myself—and must bear it as I may.
TAL. We have been good friends, Percy.
MIKE. Yes.
TAL. I have no wish to claim your confidence; but, you know, old man, if you have a trouble, it is selfish not to let me share it, isn't it?
MIKE. You can't share this.
TAL. All right. (*a pause*) Shall we have some breakfast?
MIKE. None for me.
TAL. (*brings* MIKE *down to* C., *arm in arm*) Percy, may I ask you, is your sudden departure connected with my cousin, Lady Rose Lawless?

MIKE. I know what is passing in your mind.
TAL. No, you don't.
MIKE. You think I am beginning to love her?
TAL. Yes!
MIKE. That she is inclined to encourage me?
TAL. Yes!
MIKE. And that I throw up the game because I love you, Bertie, most sincerely, and I know you have given her all your honest heart?

TALBOYS *sits* L. *of table* R.; MIKE *stands by him* C.

TAL. Oh, how truly you read it!
MIKE. And how you misread mine! Win her, if you can! Take her! She is a priceless jewel, with all her flaws! noble, with all her weakness——
TAL. Then how comes it that you have not fallen under her spell? It seems to me impossible to avoid it.
MIKE. Do you recollect one night, when you and I went to see a den of thieves under the guard of a police officer, he made us leave all our valuables at home? Well, when I entered London life I divested my breast of all its valuables. I left my heart at home in Ireland with one who takes care of all that is good and pure in my nature.

MIKE *crosses at back of table to* R.H., *by desk; looks at picture of his home on wall over desk.*

TAL. What a weight you have lifted off my life! (*bell heard off*)
MIKE. Who can that be, at this hour?
TAL. Lady Rose threatened to call here on her way to Riverside, and offered us seats in her carriage.
MIKE. She must not see the rooms in this state. Help me to repair the ruins. (MIKE *and* TALBOYS *kneel and pick up the cards*)

Enter ROMSEY LEAKE *and* CHALKER R.H.D.

ROM. (*aside, to* CHALKER) What are they doing? Playing cards on the floor?
CHAL. A rum game, governors!
MIKE. (*looking up*) Leake! (*rising*)
TAL. The devil! (*rising*)
ROM. At your service, gentlemen. (*they rise and throw the cards on the table*)
MIKE. I cannot receive you at present, sir. My lawyer has my instructions to settle your business. (*goes up* C. *to window*)
ROM. I've seen him, and can get no satisfaction.
MIKE. What do you want?
ROM. (L.C.) Our house has lent you over twenty thou-

sand pounds. Well, sir, you will excuse our anxiety, which made us send over to make henquiries as to what Walsingham you are. (MIKE *comes down* L.H. *to fireplace*) I sent over to Roscommon, where that family live, and the folks in that county says that the only Percy Walsingham they knowed died more than two year ago. You ain't that one, are you?

MIKE. (*coming down*) Be satisfied, Mr. Leake. I have never represented myself as belonging to that family. I am the only son of a gentleman whose estate, when it comes to me, will suffice to pay your loan.

ROM. But won't you tell us where these estates are to be found?

MIKE. (L.H.) You obliged me to sign a consent to judgment for the whole of my debt to you when you made me the last advance.

ROM. Yes, sir, we hold that security.

MIKE. I decline to afford you any further satisfaction.

ROM. (C) In that case, sir, I'm sorry to say I've took out hexecution on that judgment. This here is Mr. Chalker, sir! If it won't hinconwenience you, he will stop on the premises.

TAL. (R.H.) Do you mean that this person is placed here as a man in possession?

CHAL. Possession is the word, sir. (MIKE *leans on mantelpiece, dejected*)

ROM. We will begin with the next room and take a hinventory. Come, Chalker.

Goes with CHALKER *to door* L.H.U.E., *back of table* L.H.

(*to* MIKE) No offence, sir! You stand werry high in society here, there's no denying that; but no one can tell me where you come from, nor who you are! You writes pottery and are pop'lar in newspapers—that's agin your character in the money market!—young gentlemen of fortin' ain't brought up to expose theirselves and families like that 'ere!—you've got to be a lord to stand it!—but, if it be all right, why, I'm agreeable to wait! Mr. Walsingham has only to refer me to his family. Now, Chalker!

Exeunt CHALKER *and* LEAKE *into room*, L.U.E.

TAL. What does it all mean? (*crossing to* R.C.)

MIKE. It means the first step to ruin. (*comes down* L.H.)

TAL. Ruin?

MIKE. (*speaking rapidly, bitterly, and despairingly*) Two years ago I came to London from the West of Ireland,

where I left in my humble home a father who adored me
—my mother, who worshipped her only son—and a loving girl, whom I—had promised to make my wife. I
was the idol of these simple, faithful hearts—the wonder
of their little world. My father allowed me four hundred
pounds a-year when I went as a student to Trinity College, Dublin, that his boy might make, as he fondly
thought, a grand figure in the world. (*gets to centre*) It
was there I met young Percy Walsingham—we roomed
together—he was my college chum; a poor, ailing fellow,
whom I nursed during his last illness—we were sincerely
attached to each other, and it was by his bedside I wrote
my first poems and signed them with his name. Thus I
became known by it in London long before I arrived
here. (*crossing to* R.H.)

TAL. Who and what are you, then?

MIKE. (*throwing open door and pointing to name on it*)
There you may read it. Percy Walsingham and Michael
O'Dowd are one and the same person. I am the son of
a fish salesman in the Claddagh, county Galway.

TAL. But, my dear fellow, you must have foreseen the
(*gets* R.C.) inevitable end to all this?

MIKE. (*gets to centre*) Yes, in two years I have wasted
in folly and vanity the inheritance my poor father has
spent his life to acquire.

TAL. Is there no possible escape? No compromise?

MIKE. None. He is so proud of the name he bears,
which I have been ashamed to own. It is the oldest in
our province. (*goes to fireplace,* L.H.) The last of an old
race, a poor fisher-boy, he plied his trade under the cliffs
our family once owned. He saved and starved, until
acre by acre he recovered the lands that once belonged
to the O'Dowd; and stone by stone he bought back the old
ruin where he fondly believes his forefathers lived.

TAL. Can you conceal your ruin from him?

MIKE. Buried in the wilds of Connemara, he can never
learn what happens here. When I disappear from London,
who will care to trace my fate? If Romsey Leake discovers the truth, he dares not reveal it, lest my father
should disinherit me.

A bell rings.

TAL. Another visitor? (*goes to the window*) It is Lady
Rose with Mrs. Dudley Fowler. They come for us.

MIKE. Oh! join them; say I will follow you. Fortunately I keep a change of clothes at the club.

TAL. (*down to* R.C.) One word, Percy. I don't feel I
can leave you like this. I know I am not worth much;

but now you have told me your trouble I should feel like a cad if you don't let me stick to you through it. May I go with you to your home in Ireland? If it were not for Rose, I would ask to go with you to the end of the world. (*goes up for hat, comes down* R.C.)

MIKE. Yes; you shall come with me.

TAL. Thanks. (*going, returns*) God bless you, old fellow! I wish I had—— You know what I mean.

MIKE. Yes. I know you would.

TAL. All right. (*Exit* R.H.D.)

MIKE. So. This will be the last day of my brief but happy career. (*takes photograph.*) My father! What falsehood shall I tell him to account for my departure? (*kisses the portrait*) Brave, noble old heart! Ah, who will take my place at the fireside at home, and wipe away my mother's tears, and join the old folks in their prayers for the absent boy? So—that is all I shall take! (*puts photograph in his breast*) Farewell, dear old rooms! Scene of my illusions—of my folly—of my sin!

Exit R.H.D.

Re-enter ROMSEY LEAKE. *He has a deed in his hand.* L.H.D.

ROM. (*as he enters*) See here. What is the meaning of this here deed I found? They are gone (*runs to window, looks out*), there they go. Oh, dear! oh, dear! It can't be true; have I been deceived? (*down* R.C.)

Enter CHALKER L.H.D.

CHALK. (L.C.) Deceived's the word, Gov'nor! We are trespassing in this place, as sure as my name's Chalker. That paper is a lease of these rooms to Michael O'Dowd. This Walsingham is only a lodger here—in furnished apartments. We dare not touch a toothpick. (*goes to table* L.H., *and drinks wine*)

ROM. Oh, oh, oh! here's a pretty how-d'ye-do! He's got away with £20,000 of my money. It is ruin! ruin!

CHALK. Ruin is the word for it.

ROM. But his name is good still. I might find some friend in my line of business to take the paper off my hands. I would take ten or eight shillings in the pound. But who—who could give so much? Oh, dear! a drowning man catches at a floating straw—don't he?

CHAL. Straw is the word for it.

KITTY *looks in, reads name on the door* R.H.U.E.

KITTY. Here's the place, Daddy.

DAD. (*outside*) Are you sure now?

KITTY. I am quite sure; for here is our Mike's name on the dure. Come up and look. (*enters*)
DAD. (*outside*) I am coming.
KITTY. Will I read it to you? " Mr. Michael O'Dowd." There it is.
ROM. What a strange old figure! Ain't he?
CHAL. Looks as if he'd come out of a waxwork! What can they want here?

Enter the O'DOWD, R.H.U.E., *advances to* C.

DAD. R.C. Mr. Michael O'Dowd, av ye plaze!
ROM. C. There's no Michael O'Dowd here.
DAD. (*turns to* R.) What did ye tell me, Kitty?
KITTY. There are two names on the dure! but his own is one o' them. (*at door* R.H.)
DAD. Show me that.
KITTY. (*points to letters*) There it is!
DAD. Which is it?
KITTY. That one below there. (*at door* R.H.)
DAD. (*puts on his spectacles*) You are sure, now?
KITTY. I am, dear.
DAD. Then I'd like to see Mr. Michael O'Dowd if he is convanient. (*advances with* KITTY)
ROM. I tell you he is not here—and so far as we can learn he has not been here for some months past.
DAD. Ah! go on. Sure, the boy writes to us every week of his life——
KITTY. R. And his letters come from this place.
DAD. R.C. Where's the one we got before starting from Galway?
KITTY. Here it is, Daddy. (*she draws a letter from her breast*) The post-mark is London, three days ago.
DAD. (*to* ROMSEY) D'ye see that? (*to* KITTY) Which is the mark?
KITTY. There it is, July 21st, plain enough.
DAD. To be sure. Can't you rade, man alive! it's there plain enough. (ROMSEY *examines the letter*)
KITTY. (*going down* R.H. *to desk*) And here are all his things. There's the picture of our house (*sees it over the bureau*), and here, oh! Daddy, here is myself! (*finds portrait below it*), my own self; and see his writin' under it. (O'DOWD *goes to her* R.H.; *reads*) " Drawn by memory with the help of my heart.—Michael." (*she sits down overcome, half laughing, half crying*)
DAD. Let me look at it. Well, to be sure. It is, so it is! (*takes it from her*)
KITTY. (*sits* R. *of table* R.) And he all these miles away

in London. (*takes it from him, kisses it*) To be thinking of the—the—likes of us! (*sobs*)

DAD. Come, come, darling, don't go on like that before company. Hould up! be a man, Kitty. (*while they are engaged over the portrait,* ROMSEY LEAKE *stealthily opens the letter*)

ROM. L.C. Chalker, this letter is in the handwriting of Percy Walsingham. I'd swear to it! ain't this queer?

CHAL. L.H. Queer is the word for it, guv'nor.

ROM. May I ask your name? (KITTY *draws out a portrait from her breast and looks at it;* O'DOWD *looks up and goes to* C.)

DAD. R.C. O'Dowd, sir, is my name, and I'm proud of it! The O'Dowd of Suil-a-more, at your sarvice; once a Galway pilot and a fish salesman! (*takes back letter*) I am the father of my son, though you would not think it to look at me! D'ye know the boy, sir?

ROM. I can't see a likeness in you to anyone I am acquainted with.

DAD. Mike favours the mother, sir. She was a Bodkin; one o' the ould Connemara Bodkins of Bally Bodkin, divil a betther stock there is to the fore in the county Galway. Ye'll be wondherin' how one of their blood ever tuk up wid the likes of a poor an' ignorant boy that I was, but I had the good ould dhrop in me— I was the O'Dowd. (CHALKER *examines a photograph album on table* L.C. *up*)

KITTY. (*seated* R. *of table* R.) Wipe my eyes, Daddy, I'm puttin' my face against his own, but I—I—can't see him for the tears.

DAD. (*goes to her, wiping her eyes*) May your eyes be always wet wid the sweet dew of your heart, my dear.

ROM. His portrait! Have you got it there?

DAD. There he is. (*draws back as* ROMSEY *advances to her*)

KITTY. No. (*pressing it to her breast; rises, crosses to* R.) I—I ax your pardon, sir, but—but—I never showed it to anybody.

ROM. You will find his face in this book. (*he brings forward album*)

DAD (*crosses to* R.C.*; looking over it*) That's the mother! That's my Biddy. D'ye see the grand sthrain of the Bodkins in the way she carries her head? There's no lie in it, sir. The ould blood will tell. (KITTY R., O'DOWD R.C., ROM. L.C., CHALKER L.)

ROM. Here is your own likeness.

DAD. Ah! never mind me. I'd be ashamed of meself if my Biddy wasn't to the fore to make me proud of the son that bears my name. (*as* ROMSEY *turns the page*) Stop! There he is. (*points to a photograph*)

ROM. That!—that is *your* son?

DAD. To be sure; my son Mike! (*takes the book*)

KITTY. (*taking photo album, sits at desk* R.H., *looking over it;* O'DOWD *at her back*) Oh, let me see! (*she and* DADDY *examine the book, while* ROMSEY *and* CHALKER *face each other*)

ROM. (L.C., *aside*) Chalker, the young fellow is a fraud!

CHAL. (L.H., *aside*) Fraud is the word for it. But these rooms are his own, after all, so we can seize the goods here.

ROM. (*aside*) There! (*points to* DADDY) There's the goods I mean to seize. There's my hope! There's my security. The young fool has put a false name to my bills; that is fraud, Chalker! Perhaps it is forgery! The father is too proud of his name to allow his son to be indicted.

CHAL. (L.H.) He don't look as if he could pay £20,000.

ROM. (L.C., *aloud*) Your trade in Galway must be prosperous to maintain your son so handsomely in London.

DAD. (*turns to him and crosses to* R.C.) Four hundred pounds a year, sir. Divil a less! That's what he has to hould his head up high among the quality at Coort.

ROM. (*aside*) And he has spent ten thousand.

DAD. Suil-a-more is as purty a place as there is in Connaught, and Mike will have every sod of it, for he's my only son. (*goes to table* R.H.)

ROM. (*aside to* CHALKER) His only son! (*rubs his hands*) I would not take fifteen shillings in the pound. (*aloud*) I know you Irish farmers are not to be judged by the coat on your backs. You make a poor show for fear the landlord should raise the rent on you. Eh?

DAD. I'm my own landlord, sir. I wish every Irish farmer could say the same.

ROM. (L.C., *aside*) He's a landed proprietor, Chalker! I wouldn't take five per cent. off for cash.

DAD. (R.C.) It is long since I gave up the fish business. But our ould pilot-boat lies undther our windies still—she's one of the family, sir—blessings on her! We owe to her the home over our heads—and the lands of Suil-a-more (*sits* L. *of table* R.H.)

ROM. To the pilot-boat?

> KITTY *rises; crosses at back to fireplace* L.H.; *then returns to* C. *at back, looking round the room in her curiosity.*

DAD. Yes, indeed. A finer hooker never lifted her cheek

to the blast; and when I tuk the tiller and my boy Mike stud like a prince of the say at her bows, she was the happy crature, the darlin'. Well, sir. It was one wild day ten years ago. I was called out to see a Swedish ship in throuble outside the Skelleys—(the rocks, sir, they are, right fornist our cabin!) There she came, driftin' into the jaws of death—throwin' out signals for a pilot and firin' her guns of distress (*rises*) But not a man would stir out in such a say as howled and cursed on that shore. "Daddy," ses Mike to me, houldin' his hair on wid both his hands—for, sure, the wind blew his voice down his throat; "Daddy, asthore," ses he, "I can't stand and see it! Them milk-faced cowards dare not risk their lives. Come—we'll go alone." An' we did. He leapt into the hooker, shook out her foresail; I followed him into the boat, and, as she cleared the surf and she faced the gale wid us, she threw her head up, God bless her! for she was the proudest of us three that day.

Rom. (L.C.) You saved the ship, then?

Dad. (R.C.) The Lord saved it, and we did as we were bid! But they paid me six thousand pounds salvage for the cargo, and that's how we started a fortune—that has rowled up into twenty thousand in ten years' time. (*shakes hands with* Kitty)

Rom. (*rubbing his hands*) Twenty thousand!—and in land, too? Eh!

Dad. You would not think it to look at me?

Rom. I thought you Irish were so poor.

Dad. So we are. God help us!—poor as milch cows, whose milk goes to market, and whose calves are took away.

Rom. But you are rich?

Dad. Because I was my own master, working wid all my heart for my own flesh and blood, so I never measured my labour by the hour, but by my hopes. What I saw before me was a life—and not a week's wages.

Kitty. (C.) Sure, Daddy, the gentleman does not care a thrawneen about all this. He told us he did not know our Mike (*crosses to* R.H.)

Rom. (L.C.) Not by that name. He is better known here, in London, as Percy Walsingham, the poet.

Dad. (*picks up his umbrella*) Oh, to be sure! we forgot! The boy did not like to make a holy show of our ould name, wid the ballad-mongers and the likes of them.

Chalker *goes up* L.H.

Kitty. He's so proud!

Dad. So he put on any dirty English name that would not matther.

Rom. I know your son well. You will find him at the suburban willa of Lady Rose Lawless, not five miles from this place. There you will see him in his glory—the centre of hadmiration, surrounded by lords and ladies and dukes——

Dad. Kitty, d'ye hear?

Kitty. I'd rather have him all alone to myself.

Dad. Jooks! Does our Mike know a jook? Signs on it. D'ye mind that, darlin'? Oh, if the ould mother at home could hear this! Where would the place be ye spake of, sir? How will we find it? (*moves about eagerly and distracted with joy*)

Rom. I'll put you both in an omnibus that will set you down at the door (*goes up to door* R.H.)

Dad. We are beholden t'ye, sir. Come along. Jooks and ladies! My heart is in my mouth! Where's my umbrella? (*cannot perceive he has it under his arm*) We are going to see the quality coorting our Mike! Have you got your bundle safe now? Come! (*takes his hat*) Wait! wait (*he leans on a chair*) I ax your pardon, sir. It is only the happy pride that's chokin' me, and it turns my poor ould head.

Kitty. You are thremblin' all over, Daddy! (*gets* L. *of him*)

Dad. It will go by—in—a minute. It is nothin'—but a weakness. There, that does me good! (*wipes his eyes*) It is two years and more since I laid these ould eyes on him, so you see they are wake wid hunger for the sight of him. So there! It is betther to have had it out now—than be makin' a Judy of meself—before the lords and ladies and—he! he!—the jooks—ha! ha! Are you sure, sir, there's a jook among the quality beyant there? (*going up to door* R.)

Rom. Half a dozen of them.

Dad. We will give him a surprise. (*takes* Kitty *under his arm*)

Rom. Indeed you will.

Dad. He! he! We'll see him.

Rom. He will.

Dad. Jooks and ladies! Oh, Kitty, this is a great day for the O'Dowd!

Exit with Kitty R.H.D

[QUICK ACT DROP.]

END OF ACT I.

ACT II.

Riverside. Lawn and Villa of LADY ROSE LAWLESS. BERTIE TALBOYS, *seated at table* R.H., *is employed mixing a tankard of cup; the cup is a massive silver one with two handles.* WILCOX, *a servant, stands near him with salver and three bottles on salver.*

TAL. Have the boats returned yet?
WIL. Not yet, sir. Her ladyship is out in the wager-boat—coaching the club.
TAL. Coaching a club!
WIL. Lady Rose and her crew of seven ladies form an eight-oar club that is the pride of the river, sir.
TAL. Oh, lord!
WIL. Yes, sir; when they goes along, everything gives way to 'em as if they was a fire engyne. Then Lady Rose is so pop'lar with heverybody on the Thames. Yes, sir—no disrespect!—but all of 'em, from the Hoxford stroke to the Jack-in-the-water, stop and bless her 'eart as she sweeps by them. Oh! here she comes, sir.
TAL. Place that tankard in a bucket of ice, and add another bottle of soda-water to it. It is strong! (WILCOX *goes up* C. *a little*)

Enter LADY ROSE, R.H. 3E., *in jersey and boating dress.*

ROSE. Why did you not join us on the river?
TAL. (*sulky*) Because I did not care to watch you making an exhibition of yourself. (*goes to* L.H.)
ROSE. Thank you! Why don't you say a fool at once? —you mean it! You have been disagreeable all the afternoon. Wilcox, what have you got there? (*goes to him; takes cup*)
WIL. Champagne-cup, my lady.
ROSE. Just what I wanted! (*takes the tankard*) Bring me a cigarette; I am dying for a smoke.
TAL. Cigarette! Perhaps you would prefer a cigar?
ROSE. Never tried—but I will (*hands the tankard to* WILCOX, *who goes into the villa and places salver on table in villa centre; then exits* L.H.U.E.) I wish you would not expose me before my servants. (*sits* R.H.)
TAL. (L.) I wish you would not expose yourself before the world. Look at that costume!
ROSE. (R.C.) It is the uniform of our Atalanta Club. I am stroke oar of our Mayfair eight. Is it not *chic?*
TAL. Boating — smoking — drinking — hunting — *chic!*

What next! You profane your sex! Why were you not a man?

ROSE. Jolly mistake I wasn't! You ought to have been the girl! Oh, Bertie, if they had only changed us at nurse!—what a plunger I should have been! (*rises*)

TAL. You don't know how miserable you make me! (*rises, with glass in his hand, which he has taken from salver on seat under tree*)

ROSE. You are always finding fault with me! I know what will be the end of it—you will drive me to do something desperate—take a header into matrimony, perhaps!

TAL. Out of spite? (*drinks*)

ROSE. Yes; to get rid of you.

TAL. Can you be serious for five minutes?

ROSE. You know I can't.

TAL. Percy has come to grief.

ROSE. Over what? A woman, of course?

TAL. No; he is not such a fool as I am! (*crosses to* R.C.)

ROSE. That is true. (*crossing to* L.C.)

TAL. He leaves England to-morrow.

ROSE. Not for long, I hope?

TAL. Yes, for very long; perhaps for ever.

ROSE. I am very sorry, for he is a dear, good fellow, and so fond of you. You will feel his loss?

TAL. How will you feel it?

ROSE. Deeply—on your account.

TAL. Is that all?

ROSE. What more do you want?

TAL. Nothing! (*goes away, turns, and goes to her*) I beg your pardon, Rose; I thought you cared for him?

ROSE. If you had not been prowling round me all the while, perhaps I might. But you don't give anyone else a chance (*crosses to* R.)

TAL. If you really loved me, you could not take it so coolly.

ROSE. Couldn't I? (*crosses to* L.C.)

TAL. (R.C.) No; you would be as wretched as I am. *You* would prowl, and grill, and show some uneasiness about me.

ROSE. (C.) You men are never satisfied. If a girl loves you jealously, watchfully, you think it a bore. If we don't doubt you, you call us tepid. If we are miserable, you say, "Oh, Lord! is this the sort of life that woman is going to lead me?" If we enjoy it, you cry out, "Can't you be serious for five minutes?" Now, don't pull your mouth down because you have no answer ready. But, go on. What has happened to Percy? (*goes to tree* L.H.)

TAL. I am not at liberty to tell you.
ROSE. All right. Where is he going?
TAL. (R.C.) To the end of the world!—and I have almost made up my mind to go with him.
ROSE. (L.H.) You! Whatever do you expect to find there?
TAL. My self-respect. I am ashamed of the life I am leading in London. Penniless, hopeless, purposeless—what am I doing here? I am a fashionable tramp! That is all I am!
ROSE. Oh, Bertie, don't! (*comes down* C.)
TAL. I will! You know I am! I have nothing to live on! Oh, yes!—I forgot! I live on the sufferance of a tailor and the hopes of a moneylender that some day the name my father left me, hitherto borne by a race of gentlemen, and the right to go to Court and enter a score of noble drawing-rooms, will serve as a bait to catch some rich wife who will pay my arrears of board, lodging, and washing.
ROSE. Will you stop it? (*goes* R.C.)
TAL. No—I won't! There are too many such "dead beats" of good family in this city. I'll cut it! (*he walks backwards and forwards in front of stage during these lines*)
ROSE. (R.) Oh! oh! (*sits down, half crying, under tree* R.H.)
TAL. I'll go where I shall not be ashamed to work and take off my coat to do it—if I have one.
ROSE. B—Bertie!
TAL. And wash my only shirt——
ROSE. Oh, oh! you have made me cry! There, now are you satisfied? You—have made me—serious—enough—if that is what you wanted!
TAL. My dear Rose, I am indeed in earnest! (*goes to her*)
ROSE. You are not going to leave me?
TAL. I ought to go. I have tried very hard not to love you—but it is no use.
ROSE. Go on! who is stopping you?
TAL. You are the impediment. (*sits on stool at her feet*) You are rich, I am poor. I will not be a pensioner on my wife. Why, our servants would regard me as one of themselves—on better wages! Our children, to whom your estates must descend, would soon learn that their father was a dependant with less right than they to your house, which would be my lodging rather than my home.
ROSE. (*rising; goes to* R.C.) You think that is very fine! You flatter yourself you are doing the big thing!—yes, at my expense! You talk of your feelings! Has it oc-

curred to you to consider mine? You have made your life indispensable to me. And now, after obtaining the assurance that I can't live without you, you throw me over for a defect you knew all along! (*goes* R.)

TAL. You never confessed so much before. (*goes to her* R.C.)

ROSE. (R.) Confessed! confessed! What would you have thought of me if I had confessed? You would have told me not to expose myself.

TAL. (R.C.) You do love me, then?

ROSE. I am a fool to let you see it.

TAL. Rose, be generous! Give a fellow a chance! Let me go for a year or two, to—to one of those places where chaps make fortunes. Let me, at least, try to be worthy of you. I am not so—now. You don't see it—but others do. Give me two years. We are both—very young!

ROSE. Two years!——

TAL. If I fail—consider me—scratched.

ROSE. Two—mortal years!——

TAL. You are thinking that you cannot answer for yourself until I come back?

ROSE. No, quite the contrary. So I was thinking you might marry me—before you go—on the quiet.

TAL. My darling! there is an obstacle you are not aware of. I am in debt!

ROSE. I know it.

TAL. You don't know how deeply.

ROSE. Yes, I do. Your lawyer told me. Oh, Bertie, don't be angry! but I—I saw you were in trouble. I did not mean to do wrong. You are my cousin, my only relative. We were brought up from childhood together.

TAL. No matter. You went to my lawyer? Come, out with it!

ROSE. Yes. It was not his fault. I made him do it.

TAL. Do what? (*she clings to him*) Look me in the face! What did you make him do?

ROSE. I can't tell you if you look like that.

TAL. You must.

ROSE. Promise me you won't be angry.

TAL. You paid my debts? Do you hear? Why don't you answer me?

ROSE. Forgive me!—— (*puts her away*)

TAL. Let me breathe a bit. This *is* a facer! This knocks me out of time. By Jove! this floors me. I don't know whether to feel despicable or proud, happy or miserable. (*he walks up and down and gets* R.H.)

ROSE. (L.C.) Now I *am* in for it!

TAL. I can't be the bad lot I thought I was when I am loved by so good a woman. (*comes to her* R.C.)

ROSE. You don't mean *me?*

TAL. You don't know what an angel you are.

ROSE. All right. That does not interest me. But, tell me, have I cleared off the obstacles—impediments? There are no more?

TAL. You have raised one, in doing what you have done. You have become my creditor, to whom I owe a debt of honour.

ROSE. Who does not intend to lose sight of the security.

TAL. I must go, Rose, now. More than ever I must do so.

ROSE. Oh, if imprisonment for debt had not been abolished, I might have locked him up! (*turns away*)

Enter COLONEL MULDOON *and* OSSIDEW, L.H.U.E.

MUL. I bring good news—glorious news!

Enter MIKE *and* MRS. DUDLEY FOWLER; LADIES *and* GENTLEMEN *at back*, R.H.

MRS. D. F. Why, Colonel, you look radiant! What ails you?

OSSI. (R.C.) What detained you and Borromore in town?

MUL. (L.H.) My native borough, Bally-na-Cuish, has revolted. I expected to walk into the seat as usual, unopposed, but the agitators have started a rival candidate, and Her Majesty's Government suggest that I retire and make room for the only man that, in their opinion, can secure the vote, and that man is our friend, Percy Walsingham.

MIKE. (R.C.) Me!

ALL. Bravo!

MUL. I have abdicated in his favour.

MRS. D. F. (R.C.) You cannot refuse!

ALL. Refuse! No! no!

OSSI. (L.C.) It is the first step to office.

ROSE. You will be the leader of a party in the House.

MRS. D. F. (R.C.) Here's to the future Minister for Irish Affairs! (*back of table*)

TAL. (*aside*) What can he say?

ROSE. (L.C.) Ladies, we shall parade at Bally—Bally where?

MUL. Na-Cuish.

ROSE. We must canvass the borough. How many constituents are there in it?

MUL. A hundred and sixty-three.

ROSE. (L.C.) A dozen a-piece will carry him in.

MRS. D. F. But who dares to oppose him?

Mul. (*crossing to* c., *back to the audience*) The other side have unearthed an old Galway fisherman who cannot write his name, who made a fortune, I believe, by saving some vessel from wreck, and by selling haddock.

Mike. (*aside*) My father!

Ossi. What is the House of Commons coming to?

Rose. What is the creature's name?

Mul. I forget. But what name can stand against the reputation of our noble friend and the family influence of the Walsinghams?

Mike. I must decline.

All. Decline!

Mul. My dear fellow, it is too late. I have accepted the nomination for you. I penned your address to the borough before I left Pall Mall, and telegraphed it to the Bally-na-Cuish *Liberator*. It is in type by this time.

Mike. I am sorry you have done that, for it is impossible for me to accept the honour. A reverse of fortune obliges me to leave England at once, and this day is the last I can hope to call a happy one.

Mrs. D. F. You are not serious?

Mike. Indeed, I am so!

Rose. (*aside to* Tal.) Is he ruined?

Tal. (*aside to her*) I fear he is.

Mrs. D. F. (*overhearing the words*) Ruined! (*crossing to* L.C.)

Tal. Hush!

Mrs. D. F. When does he go?

Tal. To-morrow.

Mrs. D. F. Rose, I wish to speak with you (*to* Tal.) Will you pardon us? (*she takes* Rose *aside up* L.H.)

Ossi. (c., *to* Mike) Have you measured the prospects you abandon?

Mul. (c.) There is a title dormant in the Walsingham family. Your services will enable you to get it revived.

Ossi. (c.) You are mad—to throw away such a future!

Rose. (L.H., *up stage*) The tennis ground is ready. Shall we adjourn there?

Exeunt all but Mike, Talboys, *and* Rose, R.H. 3E.

Mike. Too late! too late! (*sitting* L. *of table* R.H.) Fortune seems to taunt me with these honours I cannot accept, and shows me a future I cannot embrace!

Rose. You don't know all she has in store for you. There is a break in the clouds; a gleam of sunshine appears.

Mike. What do you mean?

Rose. (*goes to him*) Mrs. Dudley Fowler is your captive. She possesses an estate of twelve thousand a year. She would not be unwilling to exchange her name for yours.

MIKE. (*aside to* TALBOYS) Would she do so—if she knew it? (*rises; goes to* c.)

TAL. (*aside to him*) Love is the soul of Mercy, and holds the bandage of Justice. She will forgive you for her own sake.

ROSE. A refuge from the storm opens its arms to you.

TAL. You are not free as I am to be ruined. I can afford it; you can't. No one is hurt by my fall, but you will crush the lives of those at home. I have no home.

ROSE. Let us go and announce that you will remain and accept the nomination; the widow will understand that she is included. Your silence means consent. Come, Bertie.

Exeunt TALBOYS *and* ROSE, R.H. 3E.

MIKE. My degradation is complete! (*sits at table* R.) To conceal my falsehood from my father, must I add to my imposture by deceiving this noble-hearted woman by accepting a love I cannot return? Must I sacrifice the girl I adore? Oh, if the world could see me as I see myself!

Enter WILCOX, *followed by the* O'DOWD *and* KITTY, *in villa*, L.H.U.E.

WIL. I assure you there is no person of that name here. Try next door.

O'DOWD. Ah! go on out of that, and let me see for meself. (*enters; to* MIKE) I ax your honour's pardon, but is there one Mike O'Dowd?—— (*advancing down* c.)

WILCOX *staggers in astonishment.*

MIKE. (*turning*) My father!

KITTY. Mike!—(*she drops her bundle*)—Mike, darlin'! (*runs to him; he meets her and takes her in his arms*)

MIKE. My Kitty!

O'DOWD. My boy—my own boy—himself—his own self! Oh! Kitty, dear, when you've done, wouldn't you lave me a bit?

MIKE. My dear father! (*he passes* KITTY *across and the* O'DOWD *embraces him*)

O'DOWD. Sure, my sowl is dhry and me ould eyes wants a long dhrink.

MIKE. You can leave us, Wilcox. (*sits* R. *of table* R.H., KITTY *on his knee*)

O'DOWD. Get out, young man, if you plaze. You wanted to turn us out, and one good turn desarves another. Come here, now. There's not a dhrop of ill-blood in the O'Dowd. Hould yer hand! There—there's twopence. Them quality futmin always expect something.

Exit WILCOX, L.H.U.E.

KITTY. (*who is sitting on* MIKE's *knee*) You are lookin' a thrifle pale, dear. Isn't he?

O'DOWD. (*at back of table*) Sure, it's the delicacy of him. Would ye have him as brown and common as yourself? Well, to be sure, my heart is in my mouth!

MIKE. How did you know that I was here? (*rises*)

O'DOWD. Two friends of your own we met at your rooms. (*crosses to* C.)

KITTY. They tould us where we would find you.

MIKE. (*aside*) It was Leake and Chalker.

KITTY. Mighty civil gentlemen! They put us into an omnibus. But how your heart is beating, Mike, aroon, and your cheeks are burnin'!

MIKE. It is only the surprise—the emotion your presence excites in me.

O'DOWD. Sure, I'd like a dhrop of wather myself to help to swallow my own heart that is chokin' me this minute. Would your grand friend, the lady here—what's her name?—be angry if Kitty was to run down to the kitchen and dhraw me a jugful o' dhrink from the pump?

MIKE. (*rises*) No; I will find it here.

KITTY. No. Let me wait on him! (*runs up to table in villa* C.)

MIKE. (R.H., *aside*) What shall I do? How get them away before they are seen by the party here? They must return to town at once.

> O'DOWD *crosses to tree seat* L., *where he has thrown his umbrella and hat; he picks them up.* KITTY, *with the tankard of cup, comes down* C.

KITTY. This is all the dhrink I can find.

MIKE. (C.; *takes cup from* KITTY, *crosses to* C., *and gives it to* O'DOWD) Drink, father; drink to the old mother in the far west at home.

O'DOWD. (L.C.) Biddy, my blessin'! My heart turns towards ye—wishes ye were here. (*drinks*) Oh, murdher! Tare-alive-oo! Biddy, here's to ye again! (*drinks*) What is it at all?

MIKE. It is cup. (*crosses to* R.H.)

O'DOWD. Cup! Well, may I never find the bottom of it. Will ye drink, Kitty? Do!

KITTY. (C.) No. I have all I want here.

O'DOWD. Where's the bundle, dear? Open the bundle for the boy, and show him the few things the ould mother put up for him. (KITTY *kneels and unties the bundle*, C.) A pair of good warm stockin's agin' the cowld weather.

KITTY. (*opening a pair of coarse woollen stockings*) I'm afeard, father, we forget that he is too fine to wear such things now.

O'DOWD. Too fine! Sure there is not a thread in them that has not been tenderly touched by the mother's fingers. The wool is spun from her heart, and the colour is fast wid her proud and happy tears.

KITTY. And here is a comforter and mittens that she made for you.

MIKE. (R.) God bless her!

KITTY. And here is a purse—from myself. But I'm a'most ashamed of it. (*he kisses her*)

O'DOWD. (*puts down tankard under tree* L.H.; *goes to* KITTY L.C.) But where is the crock of butther—our own? Ye remember it is sweet wid the breath of the cow. And have you the posy safe? It is from your own ould flower-bed you were so fond of. 'Tis Kitty's now. And in the middle of it, look, I put a sod of shamrock that I gathered from our own hill-side. I put it into the heart of the posy; and, see! it has kept the flowers alive. I knew the sight of it would warm your own.

MIKE. (R.) And so it does. But what brings you here to London so suddenly?

O'DOWD. I came to fetch you home. The borough of Bally-na-Cuish wants a Member o' Parli'ment.

MIKE. I have heard that they offered the seat to my fether.

O'DOWD. Divil a less! "Ah! go on," says I. "Don't be pokin' your fun at the likes o' me!" "Your name is enough," says they. "There's not a man, woman, or child that would not rally round the O'Dowd." Well, if I wasn't chokin' wid the pride when I heard that. (KITTY *takes up basket; gets* L.H.) "Sure," says I, "there's one that wears my name betther than ever I did, or could, and that's my son. Tare alive! Such a shout as they gave! Didn't ye hear it over here?

MIKE. Well, what followed?

O'DOWD. What followed! Sure, you know well enough.

MIKE. They left you to consult me?

O'DOWD. Divil a bit! They left me at four in the morning—God bless them!—blind dhrunk.

MIKE. (*crosses to* R.) True. I forgot. (*aside*) I am the nominee of both parties.

O'DOWD. (C.) Then I tucked Kitty under my arm and we left the shores of Galway for the first time in our lives: and here we are!

KITTY. (L.C.) Sure, we are forgetting that Mike is not at home here. We are throubling him, maybe. When he can get away from his grand friends he will come to see us.

MIKE. Do you think I could leave you? (*crosses up between them*) I shall return with you at once to London: share your lodging, wherever it may be. Remain here until I find you a conveyance. (*aside*) Thank Heaven the party are engaged at their lawn-tennis! (*going up* C.)

Enter WILCOX, L.H.U.E.

Wilcox, where shall I find a cab near here?

WIL. You will be sure to find one at the " Pigeons," sir.

Exit MIKE, L.H.U.E.

O'DOWD. Let us take a good look at this grand place, Kitty, while we have the chance. Well, to be sure! Did ye ever see the like? (*puts on his spectacles and goes into villa* c.)

WIL. (*aside*) Who can they be? They were very familiar with Mr. Walsingham. Poor relations, maybe.

O'DOWD. The tables are made out o' goold itself, and there's satin petticoats on the dures and the windies, my dear. Well, well! And our Mike is let in to see all this grandeur—and, bedad, sir! he thinks nothen' of it: he takes to it like a young duck to the wather. (*a roll of thunder is heard*) What is that?

KITTY. It is a thunder-shower that is coming.

O'DOWD. I'm so shut up here in London. Upon my conscience, I can't see what is coming!

Enter TALBOYS, MRS. DUDLEY FOWLER, COLONEL MULDOON, LADY ROSE, OSSIDEW, BORROMORE, MAUD, *and* LADIES, R.H. 3E.

MAUD. We have just escaped the storm.

MRS. D. F. These trees will afford us shelter enough.

O'DOWD. Here come the ladies and the jooks.

MAUD. It will pass over.

MRS. D. F. Where is Mr. Walsingham?

TAL. Who are these extraordinary people?

WIL. (*aside to him*) They are friends of Mr. Walsingham's. Poor relations, I think, sir, come a-beggin'.

KITTY. (*aside to* O'DOWD) Come away, Daddy.

O'DOWD. What for? Sure, them's the quality! My sarvice to you, ladies. Lave my coat alone! What's the matther wid you?

KITTY. I'm afeard!

O'DOWD. Where's your manners?

Rose. Where did they spring from?
Mul. Escaped from a menagerie.
Ossi. Or the waxwork of Madame Tussaud.
Mul. What a queer pair!
O'Dowd. D'ye mind how they look at us?
Kitty. Yes, Daddy, I do.
O'Dowd. I'll go bail, now, ladies, you'd never be able to guess who is to the fore. He! he!
Mul. Is he drunk?
O'Dowd. Well, I may as well tell ye my name at onst I am the O'Dowd.
Tal. (R.H., *aside*) The father of Percy! Oh, the devil!
O'Dowd. (L.C.) Yes, indeed! You would not think it to look at my son Mike. Him so grand!—just like one of yourselves!
Ossi. (*aside*) Let us humour the old fool.
Rose. But how came they here?
Tal. The rain-storm must have driven them to seek shelter in the hall. Let me explain to them their mistake and send them away.
Mul. No. Let us have some fun out of the old fellow first. (*gets tankard from under tree, L.H., and offers it*) May I offer you some refreshment?
O'Dowd. I'm behoulden to you—but I believe I've finished it.
Mul. (*looking into it*) He has! That is cool!
O'Dowd. True for ye, sir—it was—and pleasant.

Muldoon *puts tankard back and sits under tree,* Maud *by him.*

Mrs. D. F. (*seeing articles on table*) What on earth have we here? (*back of table, R.H.*)
Rose. Wilcox, what is this rubbish? Take it away!
Kitty. No. (*runs across*) It is ours. I beg your pardon. We did not mean to offend, or to intrude.
Ossi. The girl is nice!
O'Dowd. This is my niece, Miss Kitty McCoul, of Bally-ma-coul, one of the raal ould Connemara breed.
Kitty. (*aside to him*) Oh, Daddy, do come away.
O'Dowd. Sure, them's the quality Mike spakes about; and, if they are proud of him, would not they be glad to know us?
Tal. (R.H., *aside*) Where can Percy be? Has he escaped from this exposure?
O'Dowd. It is blood that tells in the long run. Look at me! I'm proud to own I had no book-larnin' when I began life—a poor boy betune the two shafts of a thruck,

and drew fish to market. Did Mikey never tell yez about that?

ALL. Ha! ha! ha!

MRS. DUDLEY FOWLER *sits* R. *of table* R.H.; ROSE *sits* L. *of table* R.H.

MUL. No. Mikey gave us no fishy details.

TAL. (R.H., *aside*) I am on red-hot coals!

ROSE. (R.C.) It is a shame to ridicule the poor old man.

KITTY. Oh, do come away! (*seated* L. *of table* R.)

O'DOWD. The boy is proud of it: and small blame to him; for he knows how hard his mother and myself worked, and sthrove, and slaved to put shillin' on shillin' for our only one, that he might rise to be the gentleman he is. So we sent him to a quality school—£60 a year, if ye plaze!—an' afther that to Thrinity College, Dublin. 'Twas £300 a year he stud me in, divil a less! fur the Latin and furrin matchemattics, and a coorse of all the knowledgeables. And now he gets £400 a year—£100 every quarther-day—to kape up his head here amongst yerselves at Court—grandees, and lords, and ladies, and jooks. He! he!

ALL. Ha! ha! ha!

OSSI. (*aside*) The old fishmonger is splendid! (*seated under tree* L.H.)

MRS. D. F. (*aside*) What a strange creature!

O'DOWD. I ax your pardon—but would it be axin' too much to know which is the duke amongst yez?

MUL. (*brings* OSSIDEW *down from* L.H. *to* C.) The duke— oh, of course! (*presenting* OSSIDEW) Let me present you to the Duke of Airshire.

O'DOWD. Stop, now! (*crosses to* R.C.; *puts on spectacles and looks at him*) We av only got one jook in Ireland, and maybe I'd never get a chance to see another. Well, to be sure! I'd never have tuk him for more than an or'nary man!

OSSI. This is the Duchess of Piccadilly; and that lady is the Countess of Covent Garden.

O'DOWD. My respects to your ladyship. Oh, Kitty, isn't this grandeur?

Enter MIKE *through the villa; he stops on seeing the group,* L.H.U.E.

TAL. (*to* ROSE) For heaven's sake rescue this poor old fellow from this painful scene!

BORRO. (*aside to* OSSIDEW *and* MULDOON) I will wager you that I kiss the girl under the old fellow's nose, and he will be proud of it!

Ossi. (*aside*) Done! For a tenner!

O'Dowd. And may I ax, sir, who you are yourself?

Borro. I am the hereditary Prince of Rosherville, entitled to wear my hat in the presence of Royalty, and to salute all the fair ones who are presented to me. Allow me to exercise my charming privilege. (*advances to* Kitty, *who recoils*)

Mike. (*advancing* L.C. *quickly, takes* Kitty's *hand*) This lady is my affianced wife, my lord.

All. Your wife! (Mrs. Dudley Fowler *sits*, R.H.; Borromore *laughs*)

Mike. And I allow no man to address her with his hat on. (*going up to him* C., *points to* Borromore's *hat. After a pause*) Remove it, or will you compel me to do so? (Borromore *removes it*)

Rose. Mr. Walsingham, you forget yourself! (*crossing to* R.C.)

Mike. No, Lady Rose; but I have forgotten myself until now. (*down to* L.; *takes* O'Dowd *by the hand, and leads him up* C.) Let me present you to my father.

Mrs. Dudley Fowler *crosses at back to* Kitty, L.H.

O'Dowd. My sarvice to your ladyship—(*crosses* Mike *to* C.)—an' when I see so much beauty an' sweetness around me this minute Kitty should feel mighty proud indeed that our Mike has stud his ground agin' yez all.

Enter Wilcox, L.H.U.E., *who speaks to* Ossidew, R.C.

Mike. (L.C., *aside to him*) Father, for heaven's sake be silent!

O'Dowd. (C., *aside to him*) Warn't you too hard on the Prince wid the hat?

Wil. The gentleman's cab is waiting.

Ossi. Mr. O'Dowd's four-wheeler stops the way.

All. He! he!

Rose. (*advancing from* R.) Will you accept seats in my carriage? I shall feel pleased to take you back to town with me.

O'Dowd. Is it me—me sit beside yourself?

Mrs. D. F. (L.H.) I hope Miss McCoul will accept my hand. My carriage is at her service.

Rose. (R.C., *to* O'Dowd) Where do you reside in London?

O'Dowd. (C.) Wid a relation of my own, my lady, that kapes a very dacent house in Spitalfields—the "Pig and Whistle," by Owen O'Dowd. (Mrs. Dudley Fowler *crosses to* L., *giving her hand to* Mike)

Rose. I hope that during your stay in London you will remain with me as my guests.

O'Dowd. Is it live in your house and see your sunny

face every day? Indeed, and I will, wid a heart and a-half!

ROSE. (L.C.) Won't you offer me your arm?

O'DOWD. (R.C., *aside*) Oh! why can't I be outside and see myself going by? (*as he walks round*)

> LADY ROSE, *leaning on the arm of the* O'DOWD, *goes up the stage. As they go up,* O'DOWD *sees the* SERVANTS; *puts his hand in his pocket;* MIKE *restrains him. The* LADIES *and* GENTLEMEN *separate and bow to them.* MRS. DUDLEY FOWLER *follows, with* KITTY *and* MIKE. *Ring down when* O'DOWD *puts his hand in his pocket to give* SERVANTS *coppers.*

[TABLEAU.]

END OF ACT.

ACT III.

> SCENE I.—*A Street in Bally-na-cuish; election bills all over scene; hustings centre to wall. A crowd of men, women, and children. The houses are covered with placards:* "Vote for Muldoon," "O'Dowd and Ourselves," "Now or Never," &c. BARNEY TOOLE, MAT MORRISEY, SLIGO DAN *lead the mob. Noise, music, uproar.* MRS. DUDLEY FOWLER *at door of house* R. *Enter* LADY ROSE, *followed by man and woman from house,* R.H.

ROSE. Another vote gained. (*to* MRS. DUDLEY FOWLER) Book Terence O'Grady for the O'Dowd. (MRS. DUDLEY FOWLER *writes on note-book*)

BARNEY. If Terry had gone agin' us we'd have made a widdy of the woman that owns him. (*uproar*)

Enter THE O'DOWD *from the* C. *house.*

O'DOWD. Who said that? (BARNEY *and* DAN *run behind mob* R.H.; MAT *runs behind crowd* L.H.) Arrah, boys! would you spoil the proudest day of my life? Sure, there is a score of beautiful English ladies come over from London to see the savages they are tould we are. Who is it that wants to disgrace the county? I've got my eye on ye, Mat! Don't be hidin' that dirty face of your own in the crowd, and bad cess to yé! There is

Sligo Dan. Dan, why didn't ye lave yerself at home when ye came here? Come out and face me, Barney Toole, ye thief of the world! Stand out, I tell ye! Bate them out till I see them! (*the two men advance*) Now, listen to me, ye two vagabones! I know ye well! You don't rent a sod of turf! Divil a thatch ye have over yez but the hair on yer heads! You have no votes!

BARNEY. (R.C.) We have! We have got seven!

O'DOWD. Where are they? Blind dhrunk behind a stone wall?

BARNEY. (L.C) Gorra, he's a witch!

O'DOWD. (C) If I let yer stop here, will ye be paceable?

DAN. (R.C.) We will. ⎫
BARNEY. Never fear, O'Dowd. ⎬ *together.*
MAT. We'll be aisy. ⎭

O'DOWD. You won't let anyone else be making throuble?

ALL THREE. No, never fear! Whoo!

O'DOWD. You'll promise me now if any other blackguard rises his arm you will break his head?—for I'll have no violence, d'ye mind me?

ALL. Hurroo!

O'DOWD. (*to* LADY ROSE) Sure, they are only afeard of frightening yerself.

ALL. Here comes an opponent! Oh! (*murmurs in the crowd*)

> Enter six policemen, *escorting* MULDOON, BORROMORE, *and* OSSIDEW; *band following playing* "Croppies Lie Down," L.H. 1E.

ALL. Yah! ah! ah! Down wid the castle hack! Yah!

O'DOWD. Aisy, boys! Ordther! Where's your manners? Behave! (*The procession enters the house* C.; *policemen remain outside on guard*)

O'DOWD. (*taking* LADY ROSE *up*) Don't be afeard. They are as gentle and tendher as young ducks, and would not harm a hair of your head!

ROSE. They might harm a good many of their own.

BARNEY. Horroo, boys, here comes the young masther! (*band outside plays* "Garry Owen.")

> Enter LADIES, *escorting* MIKE *and* TALBOYS, L.H. 1E.

ALL. Hurroo! hurroo! hurroo! (*they file into centre door. The bands remain* R. *and* L. *The ladies ascend and appear at window,* R., L., R.C., *and* L.C. MULDOON, THE O'DOWD, *and* MIKE *advance on hustings* C.; BORROMORE, TALBOYS, OSSIDEW *with them at window* C. *Tumult in crowd; various cries*)

O'DOWD. Ordher, boys! Will you be quiet? What

will I do wid yez at all? Bad luck to ye! How will I stop their mouths at all? (*leans over and addresses the band*) Play up "The Rocky Road." (*the band plays* "The Rocky Road." *The crowd, gradually influenced by the air, begin to dance, and cease to shout*) D'ye see that, now? Only give them the tune they want and divil a ha'porth of harm is in them. They are only full of sport. Whoo! Aisy now! that will do. They are quiet and paceable. (*music ceases*)

Ossi. (*coming forward*) Gentlemen——

O'Dowd. Hear, hear.

Ossi. I beg to propose to you Colonel Manus Muldoon, of Ballyporeen, as a fit and proper burgess to represent this borough in Parliament.

Borro. I second that nomination. (*mingled cries*).

O'Dowd. Boys and fellow-countrymen, I offer yez my son, Michael O'Dowd, of Suil-a-more, to stand up for Ireland and Bally-na-cuish: and divil a better stander you'll find from Derry to the Fastnet Rock! I know it, for I made him myself.

All. Hurroo!

Tal. I second the nomination.

All. Up wid The O'Dowd! Galway for ever!

Muldoon *comes forward.*

Mul. My friends——

Barney. (R.C.) Divil a friend you have here!

Dan. ((L.C.) I'd like to see the crown of one!

Mul. Neighbours——

Barney. He is mighty neighbourly now he wants something.

Mul. I was born amongst you. You all know my family.

Barney. We do—and you are disgrace to it!

O'Dowd. Hear, hear!—he is! Ordher! behave!

Mul. You knew my father well?

Barney. We did—on rint-days! (*laugh*)

Mul. Did he ever distress you for the dues?

O'Dowd. No—'twas the Jews distressed him.

Mul. Did I ever turn out a tenant?

O'Dowd. The mortgagees saved you the expense. (*laugh*) Ordher, ye divils!—chair! Don't spile the speaker!

Mul. Ireland, the land of my birth, is in trouble. My heart bleeds for my country!

Barney. That's more than your pocket ever did.

Mul. The evil we have to contend with is your extravagant tendency to over-population.

All the Women. No! no! Oh, the villain! D'ye

hear him? Throw him over! Give me hoult of him! Hoo!

O'Dowd. Aisy, my jewels! (*to* Muldoon) You have done it now!

Mul. I am not to be put down! I repeat it. There are too many mouths here.

Barney. One too many! Shut your own! (*laugh*)

Mul. (*shouting*) I say the country is unable to support us all.

Barney. Not when the likes of you is out of it. (*laugh*)

Mul. The mother is unable to nurse so many children. I will be heard!

O'Dowd. Divil a sowl is spakin' barrin' yerself. (*laugh*)

Mul. I repeat it! Where was I? I have nothing to say against the rival candidate. He is a gentleman. I say I have nothing to say——

O'Dowd. Then say it. (*cheers from the mob.* Muldoon *tries to speak; the band play* "St. Patrick was a Gentleman." Muldoon *subsides, unable to gain a further hearing.* Mike *comes forward; cheers; the* Ladies *wave their handkerchiefs*)

Mike. My friends.

O'Dowd. Now you will hear something worth getting by heart. Go on, Mike, avich!

Mike. You all know what I am. The only claim to your consideration I prefer, my only title to your notice, is that I am my father's son.

O'Dowd. Don't be makin' so little of yerself!

Mike. It is in your power to place me in a position where the highest honours in the land are within my reach, but no office, no title, could raise the name which my father's spotless life has bequeathed to me as an inheritance.

O'Dowd. Oh! murther! Spake of yourself and lave me alone!

All. The O'Dowd for ever! God bless him!

Mike. His hand has never been closed to the poor, nor his heart to the suffering. You hope I shall be like him? So do I. I will say no more.

O'Dowd. Hear, hear! I was going to call on the fiddlers to put him down!

Mike. My gallant opponent has told you Ireland cannot support her population. Fifty years ago she supported over eight millions; now there are less than five—and where did they go? And where shall we all have to go? Why to America, where they were changed on their arrival on that shore into thrifty, hard-working, invaluable citizens, the life-blood of American labour, a source of American wealth and prosperity! (*cheers*)

ALL. Hurroo! hurroo!

MIKE. A time there was ere Ireland's griefs began,
    When every rood of ground maintained its man;
    But times are changed! And now a sordid trade
    Usurps the soil and banishes the spade.
    The starving peasant leaves his cabin door
    And seeks with bleeding a heart a kinder shore.
    Unhappy land! to hastening ills a prey,
    Where few grow rich and multitudes decay!
So spoke the Irish prophet-bard a century ago.

O'DOWD. Don't believe him! He made it all himself!

ALL. Hurroo!

OSSI. Burgesses of Bally-na-cuish, I call for a show of hands for Colonel Muldoon.

O'DOWD. Divil a one!

TAL. Those who are for Michael O'Dowd hold up their hands.

ALL. O'Dowd! Hoo! O'Dowd for ever!

SHERIFF. A poll is demanded on behalf of Colonel Muldoon. (*the rival bands strike up different tunes; the mob shout and surround the hustings; tumult. Scene closed in quickly*)

    SCENE II.—*Suilamore and a distant view of the Bay.*

    Enter ROMSEY LEAKE *and* CHALKER, L.H. 1E.

ROM. Come along, Chalker. What are you afraid of?

CHAL. Heverythink! Funk's the word, guv'nor! If the people here knew I carried in my pocket a warrant to arrest young O'Dowd——

ROM. (R.C.) But they don't know it; and when they do, the law will protect us.

CHAL. (L.C.) Yes—but who will protect the law?

ROM. As we passed through the village the people looked quiet and idle enough.

CHAL. Last year a friend o' mine, he had a bull-terrier in the dog-show. He gives that hanimal to me. When I went through the middle of a yard full of kennels to fetch that dog out, I felt pretty much as I feel now.

ROM. Look around you. I own this property.

CHAL. If you stop here, this property will own you.

ROM. The fields are fat with cattle and with crops. They are all mine. I never felt the sense of property before. Ain't the air sweet? Ain't the sun brighter here? It is *my* air and *my* sunshine!

CHAL. I'd rather have half a hacre in Bermondsey and a bellyful of London fog than the fee-simple of all Connemara. (*distant shouts,* "Hurroo!") What's that?

ROM. The election. The people are cheering the candidates. (*distant rifle-shots; six reports*)

CHAL. Now the police are cheering the people, I suppose.

ROM. Here comes a car full of fugitives from the town.

CHAL. Full gallop down the hill——

ROM. Something must have happened.

CHAL. Something will. They will come to smash. No! they pull up and alight.

ROM. Why, they seem to have come to smash already!

Enter COLONEL MULDOON, BORROMORE, *and* OSSIDEW, *with dilapidated clothes,* L.H. 1E.

MUL. (L.C.) Gentlemen, recover yourselves: we are beyond purshoot. Is anyone killed?

OSSI. (L.) No.

MUL. No bones broken?

OSSI. (L.) My nose feels loose.

MUL. (L.C.) Our casualties are slight.

OSSI. How did you escape? I saw a score of blows aimed at your body.

MUL. I parried them all with my head.

BORRO. I fear, Colonel, you have no chance of carrying the election. You had better retire.

MUL. When a Muldoon fights he dies, but he never surrenders!

BORRO. I'll bet you one thousand pounds to one you are defeated!

OSSI. One thousand to two——

ROM. I will take your bets, gentlemen, and I book them. (*crossing to centre*)

MUL. Who the devil may you be?

ROM. (L.C.) Romsey Leake, sir: Hart Street, Bloomsbury. Clergymen, officers on full pay, and gentlemen in Government offices requiring of temporary assistance can be accommodated on reasonable terms with loans on their own personal security. (*hands cards round*) I knows you all, gentlemen. One thousand to two with you, my lord Borromore—booked it is!—one thousand to two with you, sir: two thousand to three! The Colonel shall hold the stakes.

OSSI. (R.H.) But who's a-goin' to hold the Colonel?

ROM. I believe, sir, you are a magistrate of this county?

MUL. I am, sir.

Rom. Then I would ask these gentlemen to allow me a few minutes in private with you.

Ossi. We will stroll on to the house and repair damages.

Mul. Stop! I perceive this man's game. He has got £2,000 on the event. With this amount he can buy up one hundred votes at £20 a-piece. Oh, why didn't I think of that when I was in London? I was so unpopular! I could have got any odds against meself!

Rom. Don't be alarmed, gentlemen. I pledge myself not to spend one shilling in bribery. I shall simply oblige Mr. Michael O'Dowd to withdraw from the contest.

Mul. What! Strike his flag in the moment of victory?

Rom. And surrender unconditionally. Will the gentlemen oblige me by leaving us together?

Exeunt Borromore *and* Ossidew, L.H. 1E.

Mul. (*crossing to* L.H.; *calling after them*) You will find the materials on the sideboard if my committee has not got there before you! (*to* Rom) Now, sir?

Rom. (R.C.) Mr. Michael O'Dowd is in my debt to an amount to over £20,000.

Mul. (L.C.) I congratulate the gentleman. £20,000! Well, sir, he did you credit! I got some of it. He spent it like an Irish prince. Oh, Crœsus! think of £20,000! Oh, if I had it!—why it would be £40,000 a year for six months!

Rom. I hold his bonds for over that amount, but these bonds are signed by Percy Walsingham.

Mul. What d'ye mane me to understand by that, sir?

Rom. Chalker, give me that warrant. Here, Colonel, is something that requires your signature as a magistrate to enable us to put it into force. (*hands* Muldoon *a paper, which he reads*) I obtained that in London on a hinformation laid against Michael O'Dowd for forgery, and for obtaining money under false pretences. Felony, sir, that is what it is on the face of it. He don't know it: he did not mean it. But that is no odds—felony it is. Ain't it, Chalker?

Chal. (R.H.) Pentonville is the word, guv'nor.

Mul. You propose I should sign this warrant to arrest my opponent?

Rom. Don't you see the move? You get the seat and I get £2,000.

Mul. And you have the effrontery to make me such an offer?

Rom. Well, if you think you ought to have some of the

money, I'll share with you—there! I can't say fairer than that.

Mul. You half-bred son of a Mile-End costermonger, do you dare to bring such a proposition to a Muldoon? (*he throws the warrant at* Romsey) See, now. If in one hour from this time you are found on the barony there won't be enough of aither of you left to hold an inquest over. Your errand here shall be known. So take one hour's start, and run for your dirty lives.

Chal. Start is the word, guv'nor.

Rom. I'll take the law of them that assaults me.

Mul. Ain't I giving you one hour's law?—and it goes against my conscience to do that. But I am a magistrate, and so, out of respect for the commission of the peace, I will wait one hour before I lay the boys of Suilamore on your scent. (Romsey *picks up the warrant*) Be off, I tell you, before the tenants of The O'Dowd revenge the insult you have offered to a Muldoon. (*exeunt* Chalker *and* Leake, r.h.) He has carried off the warrant. That manes trouble for my opponent. I'm sorry I promised him an hour's law; but my word is pledged. I'll put my watch on forty minutes. (*exit* r.h. 1e.)

Scene III —*The Old Hall at Suilamore.* Kitty *is employed* l. *at a table making wheaten-meal cakes; a large yellow bowl, meal-tub, jug, and salt-box on table.* Molly *is cleaning plates.* Sheela *is folding linen. Two farm girls cross from* l.h.d., *one bearing a ham on a dish, the other a turkey. A third girl brings on a kish of turf for the fire,* r.h.

Enter Bridget O'Dowd, r.h.d.

Bridget. Hurry, now, girls. I have finished making the hall inside as fine with bushes and with flowers as our chapel is at Easter. But it can't be too fine for my boy. What is kaping him so long on the road home? (*goes up* c.)

Kitty. (*back of table* l.c.) Sure, there is not a crature he meets but stops him wid a blessing. Them that is born to be loved belongs to everybody.

Bridget. (*sits on chair* r.h. *before fire*) There is mighty little left for me. Since he came home three weeks ago I have not had him to my own self for a blessed hour together. Of an evening you carry him off, the Lord knows where! And then his father is up by sunrise to watch for him, and the minute the boy is out of his bed he whips him off from me to see this and to admire that. One would think I had no call to him at all. It's mighty hard on me, so it is! (*wipes her eyes on apron*)

KITTY. He is so proud of his son.

BRIDGET. That's all he ever did for him. But I bore him, I nursed him, and watched him. He was the love I had for the father put into flesh and blood. He was the best of me. They tuk away my white-haired boy and made a man of him.

Enter LADY ROSE, MRS. DUDLEY FOWLER, MAUD, *and* TALBOYS L.H.D.

KITTY. Oh, millia murdther, here's the quality! (*goes* C.)

BRID. What will I do? I'm making a judy of myself! (*crying*)

ROSE. (C.) We come to wish you joy.

TAL. With all our hearts.

KITTY. We ask your pardon; we do be so ashamed of how you find the place. (*goes back behind table* L.C.)

ROSE. Are you preparing for the feast in honour for your son?

TAL. Killing the fatted calf?

MRS. D. F. (C.) And you have a dance afterwards, for I see the fiddlers at the gate.

ROSE. Cannot we help you? (*goes to* L., *gets back of table* L.C.)

MRS. D. F. I will fold the linen.

ROSE. Will you let me try my hands at the cakes?

KITTY. Ah, yours were never meant for such work.

ROSE. I have a notion to emigrate to the Bush, I must learn how to make dampers. (*she turns back her dress and puts on an apron*)

MAUD. (L.T.) I'll wash the plates.

TAL. (R.C., *looking round*) What shall I do?

ROSE. Milk the cow. (*he takes up a dish cover*)

KITTY. You will want more buttermilk.

TAL. (*gets dish cover from dresser at back* R.H.) Which of the animals yields that article? (*the girls laugh; shouts outside*)

BRID. Here they come!

Enter THE O'DOWD, MIKE, *and* LADIES, *all on* L.H.D.

MIKE. (*runs to* BRIDGET) My dear mother! (*embraces her*)

BRID. (R.) What kept you so long on the road home?

O'D. (R.C.) I was showing the boy the fine place that

will be his own when you and me have tuk to our last bed, and have pulled the sod over us.

 KITTY *clears all the things off table* L.H., *puts them on dresser behind her,* L.H.

BRID. Show him your pride, Denny, and lave me to show him my heart.

O'D. Go on now, ye commetherin' ould schamer! you know you are as proud of Suilamore as a paycock of his tail. Kitty, my dear, is the table set? (KITTY *runs out, followed by the farm girls* R.) And sure the boys outside are dying to dhrink success to the new member.

MIKE. (C., *to* LADY ROSE) What in the name of folly are you making?

ROSE. I am making myself at home. I am cook.

MRS. D. F. (C.) And I am footman.

 MIKE *goes back to* R.H.

MAUD. (L.H.) I'm the butler.

TAL. (C.) And I'm the dairymaid.

BRID. (R.) There, Mr. O'Dowd, what d'ye think of your sarvents?

O'D. (C.) I think if there were many like them on hire there would be a rise in wages!

 KITTY *appears* R.H.D.

KITTY. The table is set.

 Enter ROMSEY LEAKE *and* CHALKER.

O'D. Mike shall take the head of the board.

MIKE. (*crosses to* R.C., *faces* LEAKE, *who has come down centre*) Lady Rose, will you (*as he turns he faces* LEAKE) Romsey Leake!

O'D. (R.) I remember now—sure we met the gentlemen at your house.

ROM. (C.) And you said we would be welcome here.

O'D. Wid a heart and a half. (*is going to offer his hand,* MIKE *stops him*)

MIKE. (R.C.) Stay, father, and leave me to receive these visitors. They come on business that admits of no delay.

O'D. What is the matter?

MIKE. I must see these men alone; leave us, I beg of you.

 Exeunt all but KITTY, MIKE, TALBOYS, LEAKE *and*
    CHALKER, R.H.D.

 BARNEY *appears at window* L.H.

BAR. (*aside to* KITTY) Whisht, Miss Kitty—whisper! There's the polis coming up the road from the barracks.

There's something dark in the wind. Will I give our boys the office and have them handy?

KITTY. There would be no harm, Barney—but what do you fear?

BAR. Fear? I don't know what you mane! but I hope if the polis make any trouble, I'll get a chance of kapin the peace—(*he disappears—by this time the party led by* O'DOWD *and* LADY ROSE *have gone off*, R.H. KITTY *disappears off* L.H.D. ; CHALKER *comes down* L.H., *sits in front, his hat on.* MIKE *looks at him indignantly;*)

CHALKER *takes off his hat, rises and goes to* L.H.

MIKE. What brings you here? (*Sits* R. *of table* L.C.)

ROM. I come to ask you to get your father to sign this deed, or put his mark, as he cannot write. (*Hands a paper*).

MIKE. What is its purport?

ROM. (C.) It is a conveyance of this estate to me. It will about cover what you owe me—principal, interest, costs, and a trifle over for Chalker.

CHAL. (L.H.) The charge for attendance on the bill don't include the waiter.

MIKE. And, you expect I shall permit my father to do this?

KITTY *reappears* L.H. *door.*

ROM. I expect you will; and you will put your name as witness to it (the right name this time), for if you refuse to do this you will sleep to-night in a felon's cell in Galway gaol.

MIKE. A felon's cell! (TALBOYS *advances*) (R.H.)

ROM. Here is the warrant! Oh, it is all correct. You may see it, Mr. Talboys. I have had it endorsed by the police magistrate, and he sent wid us a company of police —that are waiting close by—but I'm sure they won't be wanted.

TAL. (R.) There is nothing criminal in a simple debt.

ROM (C.) No, sir—but debts incurred in another man's name—bills signed by Percy Walsingham after that gent was dead and buried—and sums of money obtained on the credit of belonging to an old country family, which was a lie and a fraud. That's what your friend has done—what d'ye call that, sir? (MIKE *buries his face in his hands*).

CHAL. Noogate is the word for it.

BARNEY *appears at the window with* DAN, MAT, *and a Peasant—they enter by door at back* L.H.3.E.

KITTY. (*advancing and embracing* MIKE) And you mane

the old man should buy you off wid all that he has in the world.

Rom. (R.C.) There is all he has in the world! His only son! Do be reasonable, now! I've only got this chance to get paid. It must be ruin to me or ruin to him. It is hard on the guvnor. Didn't I always say it was, Chalker?

Chal. (L.H.) Nails was the word for it!

Mike. Give me time to clear the debt; I'll go abroad and earn it (Mike *rises, goes to* C.) Meanwhile, you shall have my reversion to this estate. I will sign anything—do anything.

Rom. But if you die before your father?

Mike. Is there no way? none?

Kitty. (*getting between them* C.) I have a trifle of my own, take that; won' you take it, sir?

Rom. I've got a better security.

Mike. Ay—you have! Tell him what I am! the news will kill him. His death will give you the possession you demand.

Barney *and* Peasant *seize* Romsey Leake, Dan *and* Mat *seize* Chalker.

Bar. Whisht now, and say your prayers! the divil is waiting on ye both. Masther, dear! the polis have surrounded the house, but our boys have surrounded the polis. (*Murmurs outside*)

Enter The O'Dowd, R.H.D.

O'D. What's all this?—Barney, Mat, Dan—how dare yez lift a hand again these men? (*he advances*).

Bar. Thrue fer ye, it is my fut I ought to lift agin' him.

O'D. Stand back, I bid ye. (*they release them*)

Enter Muldoon, L.H.D.

Talboys *sits on stool* R.H.

Mul. (*to* Rom. Leake.) So you are here afther I warned you off the lands. You thought the law would protect you? The polis are disarmed already—there's five hundred of the boys outside in charge of them. You are mad to throw away your lives by coming here! (Mul. *goes round at back to* R.H.)

O'D. If there war five thousand round the house, their lives are safe undher my roof. You hear me, Barney, Dan, Mat. These men are my guests, I promised them a welcome here, and they shall have it. Now, spake out, you are as safe as if you was in Dublin Castle.

Exeunt Barney, Mat, Dan. *and the Peasant*. L.D.H.

Rom. (R.C.) We want to settle all this in a friendly way.

O'D. (c) All what—what's at the bottom of it?
Rom. Your son.
O'D. What of him?
Rom. (R.C.) Let us keep it quiet. Young men will be young, and when they get to London they run wild, wild oats, ha, ha! they must be sown! The young 'uns sow and the old are obliged to reap.
O'D. What does he mean?
Mul. (R.H.) This man is a money-lender, and your son, it seems, is in his debt.
Rom. Over £20,000.

Chalker gets to R.H. at back.

O'D. My son! Are you mad?
Rom. I thought I was when I found he was going to cut and run from England and leave me in the hole.
Chal. Hooked it, was the word.
O'D. My son?
Rom. (R.C.) Mr. Percy Walsingham as he called himself. He was ashamed of your name, so he tucked that in, and so he imposed on everybody; ask the colonel, there, if he didn't. Nobody ever dreamed he was a sham till you turned up, but not till I was milked like a cow, Yes, I stood patient to be swindled.
O'D. Mike, d'ye hear, d'ye hear what he says ye do—and you don't brain him?
Mike. (*looking up*). Father, it—it is true.
O'D. No, don't let them say you were ashamed of me, say that's not thrue, avich, say you never denied the mother that bore, and the father that loved you?
Mike. (*aside*) Oh, these are the dregs of the bitter cup.
O'D. He does not answer me.
Kitty. (*kneeling at the feet of* Mike) Oh, forgive him!

Enter four Constabulary, L.H.D. 3E.

Mul. Stand at the door, Bertie. Let no one in. (*He gives a mug of water to* O'Dowd.)
O'D. There, it is over now. I'm ready to hear; what do you want?
Rom. We want you to put your name to this paper.
Mike. No, father. (*rises*) You shall not——
O'D. Hould your whisht, sit down. Go on, sir, what is it? I ax your pardon, but I am a common man, wid no book-larnin, and I cannot read what is in it?
Rom. Never mind that. Your son has read it; he knows it is all right. He knows you would not let us send him to jail as a common thief.

O'D. Oh! (*he is about to throw himself on* LEAKE, CHALKER *runs behind chair* R.)

ROM. Must I ask the officers to do their duty?

Points to officers; the officers advance with the handcuffs to MIKE.

O'D. Stand back—I'll—I'll do it!—I'll do it!

ROM. Of course you will. Nobody need know. His friends will keep it dark! (*crosses to back of table* L.H.) There's the bills and bonds. See, I put them in your hands. There's the warrant! Only make your cross there and you may tear up all the proofs against him.

TAL. They are leaving the table; his mother is coming here.

O'D. His mother! kape her back! lock the dure, give me the pen; (LEAKE *gets pen and ink from desk behind him* L.H.) don't let her see. Mother o' Heaven, it would kill her, if she knew. Where is the place?

ROM. There, just there. (*he guides the palsied hand of* THE O'DOWD *to make the mark*) That's done. Now you can take the papers, they are yours. Destroy them, burn them. (THE O'DOWD *receives the papers and vainly tries to tear them; they fall out of his hands*)

O'D. Burn, deshroy, bury them before the mother—the mother—lock the dure.

MIKE. Father! (*runs to him*)

KITTY. Oh, Daddy! don't look so wild!

O'D. Lock the dure I bid ye! She is coming!

O'DOWD *struggles in chair at table* L.H. *Enter* BRIDGET R.H.D.

BRID. What is the matter?

KITTY. We can't tell; his face is not like himself.

O'D. Where is my boy?

MIKE. Here, father, here.

O'D. Your voice sounds so far off. Where are you, Mike? don't lave me.

MIKE. No.

BRID. What ails you, dear?

O'D. Don't let the mother know; gi' me the pen, I'll do it, but kape her out, Mike.

MIKE. Father! father? do you not feel my arms around you?

O'D. Lock the dure!

MIKE. (*falling at the feet of* THE O'DOWD) Oh, what have I done!

O'D. Whisht! Lock the dure! Not before the mother—don't let *her* see this—not before the mother—not before the mother! (*speaking thickly and spasmodically; struggles to recover himself, but, struck down by paralysis, falls stark in his chair, murmuring inarticulately,* "L—lock the d—dure!")

TABLEAU.

END OF ACT III.

ACT IV.

SCENE.—*The Claddagh. Boat mast is seen moving behind wall; foresail to be hoisted before truck pulled off, as if boat sailed off. Six fish baskets containing fish for girls—three for* O'DOWD R.H.E. *Lighting. Empty sack for* CHALKER. *Another basket covered with white cloth for* KITTY. *The fish market and quays. A street in perspective. Fish-women and men, with trucks and creels of fish. Busy scene. Music.* DALY *is buying.*

SHEILA. (C.) (*carrying fish on her head in flat basket*) I'll sell ye a fine basket of haddock for seven shillings.

DALY. (L.C.) Seven shillings! What's the matter with the market this day? Fish was never so high.

BARNEY *enters.* R.H.U.E.

BAR. There's a gale in the bay, and the boats cannot get out. If the wind houlds in the Nor'-west we'll have a wild night.

DAN *enters,* L.H.2E.

DAN. The signal is up to haul our boats above high water-mark. There are two ships ashore on the Skelligs.

SHEILA. Lord help them!

BAR. Ye may say that, for not a living soul could do that same! they are beyond praying for.

SHEILA. (L.H.) Will ye take my fish at six shillings? It will be ten I'll be axin to-morrow if the storm is good to me and makes a high market!

DALY. If you will sell at four and sixpence! a basket I'll take the load.

SHEILA. Oh! musha, four and sixpence! ah, go on!

DALY. My money will keep, but your fish will spoil. I am buying for the Dublin market. I can't go beyond that price.

Enter LEAKE, R.H.U.E.

Four and sixpence, all round! will you take it?

LEAKE. (R.C.) I'll give five shillings.

SHEILA. (*to* DALY) Make it the ninepence, sir! four and ninepence.

GIRLS. Put the other threepence, Mr. Daly, and God bless you.

LEAKE. (R.C.) I'll give five and sixpence.

DALY. I can't advance a penny.

LEAKE. Six shillings! I'll give you six shillings!

SHEILA. (C.) (*turning*) If ye made it five pounds a fish I would not sell you the tail of one.

BAR. (*down* R.H.) Bat luck and the curse of Crommel on yerself and your following! There's not a beggar in Galway would take a crust of bread from your hands. (*goes up* C.)

LEAKE. I'll give yer seven and sixpence a creel—eight shillings! ten!

SHEILA. (*to* MR DALY) Well, sir, I'll take your offer—four and sixpence a creel all round.

DALY. Well, well, I'll make it four and eight.

GIRLS. Heaven bless you, sir—long life t'ye.

DALY. (*going out*) I'll lose by it.

SHEILA. The Lord will put it down to your account with the poor.

DALY. I will meet you at my shop.

ALL. More power, sir—blessins on ye— hurry now.

Exeunt laughing R.H.U.E. DALY *passes off* L.H.U.E. *on the other. Two children remain seated on the ground* R.

LEAKE. (R.C) They will neither buy from me, nor sell to me. The cabin doors are shut in my face as I go by. No man will work in my fields—no girl will serve in my house. I read curses on every face.

Enter CHALKER, *he carries an empty sack,* L.H.2E.

Well, Chalker, well.

CHAL. It is of no use. There is not a shop will take our money for a pound of meat or for a loaf of bread.

LEAKE. Could you not find a place where we were not known?

CHAL. (L.C.) No—the people told one another as I went along—the curse went ahead and spread around me.

LEAKE. (R.C.) Oh, if I could sell Suilamore, and get out of the county, but there is a blight on the land. All I have is in the place—and there I am in a prison, with every man and woman in the county as my gaoler.

The two children rise (*crossing to* C.).

CHAL. Black-hole is the word for it.

CHILD. One halfpenny, sir; we have not tasted bite or sup this blessed day.

Enter BARNEY *carrying a hod,* L.H.2E.

LEAKE. Poor little starvelings, there is twopence! go buy yourselves a loaf of bread!

BARNEY. (*to the children*) Did ye ever hear tell how the O'Dowd was dhruv from Suilamore and turned out to die in a ditch?

CHILD. I did—yes.

BARNEY. (*points to* LEAKE) That was the man that done it. [*Exit* R.H.U.E.

CHILD. Oh!!—(*The child looks at* LEAKE, *drops the money, and taking the other child by the arm, goes out*).

LEAKE. Even the beggar will not take charity at my hands. (CHALKER *picks up the money*)

Enter KITTY *with a basket on her head, another on her arm.* L.H. E. *She has a shawl on her head.*

CHAL. Maybe the girl does not know me. I'll speak to her. (*To* KITTY) What have you got there?

KITTY. (L.C.) Butter, eggs, fish, and wheaten-meal cakes (*puts down her basket*).

LEAKE. (*aside*) 'Tis all right—she's a country girl and does not know us

CHAL. (*aside to him*) Watch, and see that no one comes.

LEAKE. Buy all she has to sell. (*goes up stage* R)

KITTY (*kneeling down beside the baskets*) And here's two chickens! what will you please to want?

CHAL. I want it all.

KITTY. (*looking up*) Ah!!! (*she stands up*) The two carrion-crows of Suilamore! Go your ways.

CHAL. The girl herself.

LEAKE. (*comes down* R., *crosses to centre*) I ask your pardon. We did not know you. You have your revenge; you sowed your curses on the land, and they have come up. The tenants have left their holdings; ruin and weeds are growing up and choking the lands and house of Suilamore; no one dares to buy the place and I dare not leave it.

KITTY. D'ye remember your own words, that you spoke to Mike when you dhrove him from that home to go across the salt says to die like a dog killed by savages beyant there in furrin' lands:—"I'll have yer birthright," says you. "It must be ruin to you, or ruin to me. I'll have my bond." Well, you have got it. What has it been to you? (LEAKE *goes up to* R.H.)

CHAL. Ruin is the word for it,

LEAKE. Come away, Chalker.

Enter BARNEY, R.H.U.E.

CHAL. (*lingering*) There is not a day's food in the house.

KITTY. Would you stoop to likes of us for pity and for help? Well! you shall have it. (*they advance eagerly*) Stop! not from me. (*she calls*) Barney, come here; go with those two men and see that they are served with all they want to buy.

BAR. No one will dale wid them.

KITTY. Say the O'Dowd has sent you to lift the bar; that will be enough. (*to* LEAKE *and* CHALKER) Go with him.

[*Exit* BARNEY *followed by* LEAKE *and* CHALKER L.H. 2E.

'Tis getting late and the wind is rising. I must carry home all my load; it is five weary miles across the cliffs to our shanty. If I could find the O'Dowd I could put my basket on his thruck and myself betune the shafts. (*going off, meets* LADY ROSE, *who enters* R.H.U.E.) Would you be wanting any fine chickens or fresh eggs to-day?

ROSE. Kitty?

KITTY. Lady Rose! (*she staggers back,* ROSE *catches her*)

ROSE. (R.C.) My poor child, is it you indeed?

KITTY. (L.C.) I have not seen you for so long that it turned my heart over to hear your voice. (*puts down basket*)

ROSE. I bring you good news.

KITTY. About what?

ROSE. You must put down that load before I speak. Bertie is coming home from Arizona, he brings with him a fortune, one-half of which belongs to the O'Dowd.

KITTY. How can that be?

ROSE. I mean that on the ranche where Bertie and Mike were feeding cattle an old deserted mine was discovered. Experts from California have visited the place, and Bertie has sold out for £80,000; one-half belongs to his partner, Mike.

KITTY. But Mike is dead?

ROSE. I am not so sure of that. (KITTY *is about to fall.* ROSE *catches her*) Let me take the eggs. (*they come forward centre*)

KITTY. For the love o' pity tell me what you mane.

ROSE. Bertie has hopes that Mike was not killed in the fray with the Comanche Indians.

KITTY. Why does he hope it?

ROSE. Three white men were seen with the tribe by Mexican traders. One of the captives answered to the description of young O'Dowd.

KITTY. That was a year ago?
ROSE. Yes?
KITTY. He is dead or free by this time. I know his soul; it could not wear chains so long; if free he would have been here.
ROSE. We shall soon have the truth, for Bertie sailed for this port two months ago in a vessel called the *Prairie Belle*.
KITTY. And you came here to meet him? The fortune he brings comes too late. After Mike went away the O'Dowd recovered his senses and was getting to be himself again when the news of the boy's death came. The sowl of the father seemed to go away beyond the seas into the grave of his son. He lives, that is all—lives as a child, helpless, gentle. God is very good to him, for He lets him believe all the while that Mike is coming back.
ROSE. Where is he?
KITTY. Somewhere hereabouts. Come with me, I will find him. He won't know you again. Come. (*thunder, lights down, exeunt* L.H.2E.)

Enter DAN R.H.U.E.

DAN. Where is Barney? Barney Toole?

Enter BARNEY L.H. 2E.

BAR. What is the matter?
DAN. A big ship is in throuble abreast of the Skelligs; the tide caught her and she could not get about to weather Knockmahon Head.
BAR. What is her name?
DAN. (L.H.U.E.) They have got her number, it is 941.
BAR. That's the *Prairie Belle!* Just thirteen years ago in that same place, and on just such a night as this, the two O'Dowds, father and son, brought in the Swedish ship.
DAN. I mind it well.
BAR. No other men alive could save the *Prairie Belle*. They alone know the channel between them rocks called the Jawbone, where there is just sixty feet wide betune the divil's teeth sticking up on either side under wather. It is well named. If the anchors of the *Prairie Belle* won't hold her through the gale she must go ashore.
DAN. We'll go down to O'Dowd's shanty; she must lie abreast of that. Maybe we can lend a hand. (*exeunt* L.H.U.E.)

Enter MIKE R.H.U.E. *He is dressed in a sailor's suit, poor and wayworn; lightning.*

MIKE. My home! My home! so little changed. Am

I so altered that old friends pass by me and do not know me? I wanted to ask them if my father lived, but the words stuck in my throat. I feared they would recognise and curse me. (*sinks on knee* R.H.) My poor mother and Kitty, too, what has become of them? (*Enter two children* R.H.U.E.) Come here, little ones; don't be afraid of me, I am only a poor sailor, and I would not harm you. Tell me, child, is there an old man in this place called O'Dowd?

CHILD. Is it Daddy you mane?

MIKE. Daddy? Yes, dear, yes; that—Oh, my God! that childish name breaks into my heart, and—yes (*buries his face in his hands*), that is his name.

CHILD. What are you crying for?

MIKE. Never mind, but tell me, where is he? where does he live now?

CHILD. Why, we passed him and the misthress just now coming up the hill from the market. Why, there he comes now.

MIKE. Where? where?

CHILD. There. (*exit* L.H.2E.) (MIKE *staggers back to* R.H. *after looking off* R.H.U.E.)

  Enter THE O'DOWD *between the shafts of a truck, drawing a load of fish.* BRIDGET, *beside him, carries a board of fish on her head* R.H.U.E.

MIKE. (*staggering back and sinking on the ground*) My God! my father!

BRID. Asy now, Denny, and take a breath o' rest.

O'DOWD. Yes, yes.

BRID. Put it down a while.

O'DOWD. Down? oh, yes.

BRID. Are ye tired, avich?

O'DOWD. I don't know; am I?

BRID. Yes. Sit down.

O'DOWD. Yes, never fear; to be sure.

BRID. You will stop there till I come back. I'm goin' to get you a bit of the tobacco you are so fond of. Now you won't stir till I come back. Be good now.

           Exit L.H.2E.

MIKE. He has drunk the bitter cup I filled. (*He slowly approaches him and falls at his feet*) Father! father!

O'DOWD. Who? what is it?

MIKE. Do you not know me? Do not cast me from you.

O'DOWD. (*taking up two fish*) I don't know. If Biddy was here, she would tell you; you may take those two for a shillin'.

MIKE. Father, look on me, your son, your son, your boy!

O'DOWD. Don't be angry wid me, sir; sure I don't know. Biddy knows, where is she gone? Them in the basket is poor things.

MIKE. Dear father, look in my face, listen to my voice. Am I so changed? You know me.

O'DOWD. Know—know ye? No; wait till Biddy comes, she'll wait on you.

MIKE. His poor brain is gone, wrecked, shattered, and by me, by me.

Enter MULDOON *and* DALY L.H.2E.

MULDOON. An American ship is driving ashore on the rocks. (*enter* MAT *and* DAN R.H.U.E.) Are there no means of sending out asistance to her?

DAN. (R.C. *at back*) None; she lies broadside on, the holding is bad.

MULDOON. As the tide rises, her anchors will come home.

DAN. There is only one man could pilot her into the Blue Cove, and there he sits a helpless wreck.

BARNEY. (*at back; guns*) There's not a man in Galway would dar' sail through the Devil's jaws in such a gale.

O'DOWD. Ha! ha! who says that? Ye lie! there is my boy. Look how they cower down, the spalpeens; how pale they are. What, ye dar' not go? Your blood is all gone white wid fear. (*enter four boatmen* R.H.U.E.) Yes, Mike, ma bouchal, yes, we'll go; you and me alone, together. Loose her sail. I've got her, hoo! How aisy she rides the surf! Oh, the duck she is! Hould fast, darlin', hould that fore sheet till we go about; stand by and watch for the blue wather on her port bow. She knows it well, d'ye see it? Not yet? there! there it is! let all go—steady! Hould on to that! well done! She's through it like a fish. Belay that sheet and creep aft to me, ye vagabone! Is it laughin' ye are? Come under my coat, sonny, and gi' me a kiss, ha! ha! The blood of the O'Dowd never grows white wid fear! ha! ha! (MIKE *creeps to him and throws his arms over his father*)

MIKE. Father! father! (*two guns fired in succession*).

MULDOON. (*at back*) is there no hope for her. (*enter* ROSE L.H.2E.) Will no reward tempt the boatmen to try?

ROSE. (L.C.) What is the matter?

MIKE. (*recoils to* R.H.; *aside*) Lady Rose!

MULDOON. (*aside to Rose*) Yonder vessel with 300 souls on board will founder in sight of shore, if help cannot reach her within the hour. (*enter* KITTY *and* BRIDGET R.H.2E.)

ROSE. What is her name?

MULDOON. It's the *Prairie Belle.* (*gun heard*)

ROSE. No—No! (*gun repeated*)

MULDOON. It *is*, indeed.

ROSE. Bertie is on board—Bertie who brings home news of Mike.

KITTY. (*to* O'DOWD) Your son—d'ye hear, Daddy. News of your son.

MIKE. (*aside*) My mother and Kitty!

BARNEY. (*advancing* L.C. *at back*) The old pilot boat lies there by handy, the boys say if the O'Dowd will steer her, mad as he is, they will go.

ALL. Hurroo!

KITTY. He will go, if the mother bids him do it.

ROSE. (*to* BRIDGET) Will you? will you?

BRIDGET. Oh, Denny, they ask me to send you to your death.

O'DOWD. What is the matter? (*the boatmen come down to* L.H. *listening*)

MULDOON. No, the sight of the ship, the presence of the danger, the scene so like the past will serve to restore his senses. (*gun*)

O'DOWD. Them guns come from the skellies, there's a craft there in trouble. Wheer's Mike? He'll go.

ROSE. (*crossing to* R.C.) Your son's friend, Bertie Talboys is on board that ship, he brings home news of Mike—of your son. (*kneels* R *of* O'DOWD)

O'DOWD. Mike sure will go. Go fetch him. We done it before, and can do it again, wid God's help we'll do it again.

KITTY. Mike is not here.

O'DOWD. I won't go alone.

MIKE. (R.H. *aside at back*) Then *I* will! Farewell, mother! Farewell my love, my home. Father, dear father, I go to redeem my name or to bury my disgrace! (*exit up rock centre and disappears behind; wind, thunder*)

ROSE. Merciful heaven, restore his senses, give him sight to see, and sense to know our agony. (MULDOON *raises her*)

KITTY. (L.C.) See, he awakes. Daddy, don't you know this lady? (*several male and female peasants enter* R.H.U.E. *and look off at back*)

O'DOWD. Yes—I—know. Why are you kneeling there? What is all this? (*gun*)

ROSE. Don't you hear? That vessel brings home the

fortune that will restore you and yours to Suilamore. (*more peasants enter* L.H.3E. *go up and look off at back*)

O'Dowd. Mike—who tould me that he was dead?

Kitty. No, no, he lives! he is coming home. (*more people enter* R.3E., *go up to back*)

O'Dowd. Where am I? Have I been asleep?

Kitty. Yes, Daddy, that's all, a long sleep. (*more people enter and go up to back*)

Bridget. Yes, dear, a long sleep wid a bad dhrame in it. But now, you're your own man again!

Kitty. Yes! Yes! Let him see the wather, let him hear the blast; the sight of the danger will give him heart.

The crowd push off the fish-carts, and pull down the tented shed. The stormy sea and a vessel's topsails are seen by the flashes of the lightning—wind—storm —fountains of spray are thrown from time to time over back-pieces on to stage.

Dan. (*at back*) The pilot boat is gone!

Muldoon. (*running up to back*) Gone from her moorings. See, yonder she sails—a man on board of her, he is steering for the *Prairie Belle*.

Rose. May Heaven bless him, and protect him. (*exit* L.H.U.E.—*shouts*)

The mob rush up and climb the wall.

O'Dowd. That boat carries a dead man, no one but Mike and me could find the way through the Divil's jawbone on such a night, and in such a gale.

Muldoon. (*looking off*) How close he holds her to the rocks! What is he doing there?

Barney. (*at back*) Now he is abreast of the jaws.

O'Dowd. If he only knew the secret, if he knew how them jaws do open, but he will pass the channel. What does he do?

Barney. He ports his helm.

O'Dowd. (*rising*) What? What?

Muldoon. He is running the boat into the breakers— He is mad! (Kitty *runs up to back*)

O'Dowd. No, no, he is right! That's the blue channel, the secret—the secret road, he knows it. (*much agitated*) Who is the man that knows the road, who is he that takes my place?

Muldoon He is within hail of the ship.

O'Dowd. Oh, if I was there! Quick, let go your bow anchors, out wid your axes. What are they doing now?

Muldoon. They have slipped their bow cables, up goes the jib.

O'Dowd. She pays off. Her head swings. Let all go now. The tide will take her. (*topsails of ship seen to cross* L. *to* R.)

Muldoon. Mat. Barney. All's gone! Hurrah, she will be saved. (*distant cheers*)

O'Dowd. (*staggers forward*) My God! 'tis he—'tis Mike is there—none but himself could know—could do that work. 'Tis he—it is my son!

Bridget. Would to heaven it was he!

O'Dowd. I say 'tis he. You think I am mad. I have been; yes; I know it; but now I am sane. I have my senses, and I feel he is here, near me. No other could bring me back to life. No other could do what that man has done. (*re-enter* Rose L.H.U.E. *followed by crowd*)

Rose. (*down* L.H.) 'Twas Mike himself who saved the ship. (*shout*)

Bridget. My son! (Muldoon *pushes truck on one side*)

Rose. It was he who was aboard the pilot boat.

O'Dowd. Alone, alone! he done it! What did I tell ye?

Rose. He brings your fortune back.

O'Dowd. More, more than fortune, more than my senses, he brings back himself, he brings back my sowl, that has been dead without him (*cheers outside*). D'ye hear that's *h*im! his foot is ashore, I feel it plant itself upon my heart. Mike! Mike!

Mike. (*outside at back*) Father! I am here. (Kitty *and* Bridget *go up to meet* Mike *centre*)

O'Dowd. Ha! ha! ha! Mike! My boy! my boy! (*cheers repeated*)

> *Enter* Mike *centre over rocks followed by* Talboys, *he rushes to his father, they embrace*)

TABLEAU

   Mob.   *Mob.*   *Mob.*

Mat, Barney, Bridget, Kitty, Mike, O'Dowd,
Mat, Bar., Brid., Kitty, Mike, O'D., Tal., Rose, Mul.

30
1
35

www.ingramcontent.com/pod-product-compliance
Ingram Content Group UK Ltd.
Pitfield, Milton Keynes, MK11 3LW, UK
UKHW021353210325
5106UKWH00003B/36